UNMASKING THE MASK

The Spiritual Battle behind Mental Illness

DR. JAMES O. MONTFORD JR.

WESTBOW
PRESS®
A DIVISION OF THOMAS NELSON
& ZONDERVAN

WestBow Press books may be ordered through booksellers or by contacting:

WestBow Press
A Division of Thomas Nelson & Zondervan
1663 Liberty Drive
Bloomington, IN 47403
www.westbowpress.com
844-714-3454

ISBN: 978-1-6642-2088-1 (sc)
ISBN: 978-1-6642-2089-8 (e)

Library of Congress Control Number: 2021901448

Print information available on the last page.

WestBow Press rev. date: 02/12/2021

Contents

This book was originally submitted by James O. Montford Jr., at the Restoration Theological Seminar, as a dissertation on June 19, 2018, in partial fulfillment of the requirements of the degree of doctorate of Christian counseling.

Acknowledgments

I would like to thank all of those individuals who have encouraged, mentored, and supported me throughout the dissertation process as well as these last nine years through my education and internships. First, I would like to thank and acknowledge my wife of seventeen years for the previous nine years. I have worked endless nights in class online and in the classroom. Sharian, you have been supportive of this process. Thank you, and I love you for all of the support.

I would like to thank my father and mother for their words, their many words of encouragement. One of my biggest motivations is my father, who taught me to endure through his example of taking thirty-three years to complete his BA in Biblical studies—putting four of six children through college, then to retire and go back full-time to complete his degree. The words of my daddy that ring out in my ears when I start something new are "Son, don't be a quitter. Hang in there." Mama's words do too: "I know that you can do it. It's in you."

I would like to thank Ingrid Richardson, my clinical supervisor, for her words of encouragement. Ingrid never gave up on me; she encouraged me: "James, you are a good counselor." Thank you to Jamal Baker, my director and pastor, who trusted me to intern and then offered me the opportunity to stay on as a contractor counselor. He also recommended many of my clients for both professional and pastoral counseling services. I will like to thank Dr. Barbra Beeler for the door of the opportunity opened to me to complete my doctoral program and allow me to sow seeds of knowledge in several classes that I was able to teach. I would like to thank my sister, Dr. Delores Montford Davis, for reading through and marking up the dissertation. Finally, to all the students who were in my classes, your encouraging words and attendance were what I needed to come back each week and teach. I was encouraged by you to dig deeper to give you the information and make it come alive from the paper in your lives as you pursue your quest in Christian counseling and coaching.

Introduction

The concept of spiritual warfare is not new; it is foundational to the understanding of the Bible, and, indeed, it is fundamental to the myths of many early cultures. These stories arise from the need for an explanation of what is good or bad and the apparent conflict between these two qualities in nature and human functioning. However, at different times in history, the idea of spiritual warfare has reached prominence with more specific iterations of the concept of combat that include particular techniques for how to engage in this battle. It is such an iteration in our time that is the focus of this discussion. Therefore, the question to be addressed in this book is not about the existence of spiritual warfare but whether the current popular thought in evangelical and charismatic churches concerning this concept is an adequate definition of the conflict.

As a Christian counselor, I will address the curious relationship between healing or deliverance practices and mental health concerns. Let me state the approach that I have taken to this subject. In keeping with Christians throughout the ages, I do not doubt the existence of spiritual warfare, the battle between good and evil, God and Satan. I believe both good and evil are profound in their power and depth and that we must do all that is possible not to trivialize these concepts in any way. The battle between good and evil is a matter of life and death.

Several areas require discussion. The first is the cultural milieu in which the demonology of spiritual warfare is expressed. The second is the false belief that many so afflicted are mentally ill or emotionally disturbed, and third is the possible vulnerabilities of those with mental health problems, for this is the population that I know intimately.

Finally, I wish to address the question of ethics in specific spiritual warfare techniques. My perspective is the perspective of counseling and psychology and an appreciation of what science can tell us, filtered through a profound respect for the scriptures and Christ's love as expressed through His caring for us as human beings.

How then do we consider the effects of good and evil on the individual? Somewhat like germ theory in medicine, in this model, evil entities or forces enter and occupy a person (possession). In more minor forms, they are seen to merely influence a person as a force seeking expression (oppression). These models consider these influences to be a transaction primarily or entirely of the spiritual realm. One of the basic models of medicine warns against the separation of the spiritual from the other spheres of functioning. The biopsychosocial model, one of the basic models of medicine, was proposed by Dr. George Engel in the 1950s. It posits that at all times, the human being is a biological entity, a psychological entity, and a social entity. Further, these entities are in constant interaction, and each sphere of influence has an impact on all the other spheres. My view is that communication is best described as a dimensional cube where at any time and with any condition, different dimensions of each of these spheres of influence are at play.

Therefore, if I experience depression, there are biological, psychological, and social components. One or more of the neurotransmitters in the mood centers of my brain are depleted, I suffer psychologically, and I withdraw socially. It is important to note that both psychological and social remedies have an ameliorating effect on the biochemistry of depression in addition to medication. Therefore, biology is not the only driving factor.

With the growing interest in spirituality from the 1980s to present, people have added a spiritual sphere of influence to the model, making the biopsychosocial-spiritual model fundamental to the understanding of the health of the person. I don't particularly appreciate the addition of the spiritual to the model as just another sphere of influence, as in my view, it does not provide the spiritual with the force it seems to possess, for example, miracles. I prefer instead to take my cue from the ancient Greek poet, quoted by the Apostle Paul, as "The God in whom I live and move and have my being." I, therefore, diagram the spiritual as a force that permeates all the other spheres in their entirety and that cannot be clearly segregated from the others. Consequently, it is likely an oversimplification to characterize any condition as purely social or sociocultural, psychological, physical, or, for that matter, spiritual.

Spirituality is an integral and vital element in the lives of many individuals. There has been a recent explosion of studies and research in this area. Spirituality is regarded as one of the four components of overall well-being (Mohr, 2006). The four essential parts of an individual, as noted by Mohr (2006) are the physical, emotional, social, and spiritual dimensions. Spirituality may also play an essential part in the identity of an individual. People often make decisions based upon their religion and may even adhere to specific rules of living founded upon their spiritual beliefs. Research has shown that spirituality is associated with values of wholeness, hope, meaning, harmony, and transcending (O'Reilly, 2004). These values help individuals cope with stressors in the world and strive toward reaching their natural potential.

An important factor is ignored when the clinician fails to incorporate spirituality into the treatment of a spiritual individual. The research and development of several approaches related to integration have evolved over time (Richards, Rector, and Tjeltveit, 1999). These methods are relatively new, receiving mixed reviews from individuals in the field of psychology. In general, some clinicians are skeptical about the integration of spirituality and therapy, as there is a general fear that this new branch of psychology may be seen as unscientific or invalid (Lindridge, 2008). Other therapists, however, embrace this new domain and continue to work toward a healthy integration of spirituality into their practice (Shafranske and Sperry, 1990).

Many people have been acculturated through a particular kind of religious interpretation to see demons in people I would call mentally ill. I have had the opportunity to talk to people who have dealt with Christians who experience mental illnesses and their families. Many have expressed to me that the most hurtful experience is being the recipient of an unsophisticated and harsh view of mental illness by identifying it as demon possession. These ideas have been applied to people with psychotic symptoms in diseases such as schizophrenia, where hallucinations seem clearly to be the voices of evil spirits. The idea of demon oppression and possession has been applied as well to people with anxiety disorders, people with depression, victims of childhood sexual abuse, and those with any state that looks a bit strange or dramatic to the beholder. If a person is depressed, the curse is often, "If you were right with God, you would not experience this." Already people with depression are racked with guilt. They have examined themselves more cruelly than any external person ever could. It is common to name evil spirits, such as the spirit of fear or the spirit of depression. Often, these people are subjected to spiritual interventions. If and when these interventions fail, their disastrous state of hopelessness is confirmed. These people often experience an intense anger at the individuals and churches that so misunderstood them as to suggest the role of a demon.

One of the problems is that the Bible does not provide us with many clear-cut images of mental illness. There are, however, many people called "demon-possessed." A careful reading of the history of psychiatry notes that in many ancient cultures, the mentally ill were called "demon-possessed" or "possessed by spirits." It does not stand to reason that this mental disorder arose de novo after the Bible was written. Could the absence of mental illness in the Bible then suggest that some of the references to casting out demons in fact were for people with mental disorders and that the vernacular of the day was used to describe these disorders?

One concern about the overidentification of evil spirits is that within the church, those who do not respond to casting out demons may become scapegoats and be blamed for lack of faith. The responses to the idea of discrete evil spirits cause fear, avoidance, and often isolation of the person. The "diagnosis" rests with them like a rock. If they are not successfully delivered in their minds, it is evident that God is not powerful enough to heal. This is the ultimate curse that the enemy wants you to believe. This is not true; I do believe that not all mental illness can just be prayed out. This comes from fasting and praying. However, what we eat does make a difference, and I will speak on this later in this book when talking about chemical imbalance when it comes to treating mental illness. There are so many other things that we can see that can affect the mind and cause mental illness. I will talk briefly about self-induced mental illness.

Just a thought to ponder after living a life on earth in which Jesus repeatedly exercised, through the presence of the Holy Spirit, the power and authority of God over Satan and the demonic: He fulfilled His mission of the cross and His resurrection. Prior to ascending to heaven, Jesus's mandate to all believers was quite clear, as noted in Matthew 28:18–20 (ESV):

> And Jesus came and said to them, "All authority in heaven and on earth has been given to me. Go therefore, and make disciples of all nations, baptizing them in the name of the Father, Son, and Holy Spirit, teaching them to observe all that I have commanded you. And behold, I am with you always, to the end of the age.

The believer's life is all about evangelism, taking the good news of Jesus Christ to all people groups throughout the world. Jesus also made it clear that to fulfill this commissioning, His disciples would need "power" from heaven in the form of the person of the Holy Spirit. Only believers have the Holy Spirit living within them. Why is it necessary to have the presence of the Holy Spirit within the believer? As the apostle Paul explained quite clearly, the believer is thrust into the midst of a spiritual battle that will only be conclusively won with the events beginning with the second coming of Christ. As all followers of Jesus await His return, they are instructed to

> put on the whole armor of God that you may be able to stand against the schemes of the devil. For we do not wrestle against flesh and blood, but against the rulers, against the authorities, against the cosmic powers of this present darkness, against the spiritual forces of evil in the heavenly places. (Ephesians 6:11–12 ESV)

Only soldiers need armor. Christians must embrace the Scriptural truth that they are born again into a spiritual battle and that the Lord has equipped born-again believers with the Holy Spirit.

The term *spiritual warfare* can be acknowledged and further defined upon the review of many scripture passages, among them 2 Corinthians 10:3–4 ESV, "For though we walk in the flesh, we are not waging war according to the flesh. For the weapons of our warfare are not of the flesh but have divine power to destroy strongholds," and Ephesians 6:12 ESV, "For we do not wrestle against flesh and blood, but against the rulers, against the authorities, against the cosmic powers over this present darkness, against the spiritual forces of evil in the heavenly places." Both of these statements were written by the apostle Paul and clearly point to a "war" with things not of the "flesh" but "spiritual" in nature.

Spiritual warfare essentially encompasses Satan's rebellion against God and the manifestations of that rebellion in the created order. At the heart of this warfare, however, is the fact that God is sovereignly in control of His creation, and as the Sovereign One, He has already decided that Satan's rebellion will fail. The threads of Satan's rebellion and God's loving response are interwoven through the scriptures as an ongoing drama played out on the stage of human history.

"Spiritual warfare" involves two sides: God, the Father, Son, and Holy Spirit, His angels, and His human followers on the side of good and Satan, his fallen angels, and his human followers on the side of evil. Satan's rebellion against God took a significant blow and utter defeat upon the entrance and life of Jesus in this world. Throughout His life on earth, Jesus repeatedly exercised His divine authority over the demonic, culminating with His finished work on the cross and subsequent resurrection. Jesus is said to have "disarmed the rulers and authorities and put them to open shame, by triumphing over them" the cross. Col.2:15 KJV. Upon His ascension, followers of Jesus, through the indwelling of the Holy Spirit within them, pick up the fight against the spiritual forces of evil where Jesus left off. E. M. Bounds describes the Christian life this way: It cannot be said too often that the life of a Christian is warfare, an intense conflict, a lifelong contest. It is a battle fought against invisible foes who are ever alert and seeking to entrap, deceive, and ruin the souls of men. The Bible calls men to life, not a picnic or holiday. It is no pastime or pleasure excursion. It entails effort, wrestling, and struggling. It demands putting out the full energy of the spirit in order to frustrate the foe and to come out, at last, more than a conqueror. It is no primrose path, no rose-scented flirting. From start to finish, it is war. The Christian warrior is compelled from the hour he first draws his sword to "endure hardness, as a good soldier" (2 Timothy 2:3).

Chapter 1

SPIRITUAL BATTLE IN THE MIND OF THE COUNSELEE OR CLIENT

There are no answers or quick fixes for the kind of brokenness that psychiatric mental illness disorders describe. People who have been labeled with disorders like obsessive-compulsive disorder (OCD), post-traumatic stress disorder (PTSD), bipolar disorder, attention deficit hyperactivity disorder (ADHD), schizophrenia, borderline personality disorder, manic depression, and many other mental disorders are faced with real struggles and the complexity of personal and interpersonal problems. What do these diagnostic labels mean for strugglers and for those who want to help them? How should we understand the use of medication in the care of psychiatric problems from a biblical perspective? Is there any help to be found in the various secular counseling approaches? What goes into restoring and rebuilding a life? These are essential questions because a person struggling with all-consuming and complex problems needs wise help.

Statistics released in 2012 show that every year, about 42.5 million American adults (or 18.2 percent of the total adult population in the United States) has some mental illness or enduring condition, such as depression, bipolar disorder, or schizophrenia. According to the National Institute of Mental Health (NIMH), approximately one in five youth aged thirteen to eighteen (21.4 percent) experiences a severe mental disorder at some point during his or her life. For children aged eight to fifteen, the estimate is 13 percent of children with prevalent mental illness disorders.

These data, compiled by the Substance Abuse and Mental Health Services Administration (SAMHSA), also indicate that approximately 9.3 million adults, or about 4 percent of those Americans ages eighteen and up, experience "serious mental illness"—that is, their condition impedes day-to-day activities, such as going to work. In 2012, SAMHSA released that 45.9 million American adults, 20 percent of this demographic, experienced a mental illness at least once annually. Knowing that all data have to be proven, there is about a 1.8 percent difference. The statistics do have margins of error, and methods of compiling them are often revised, so this dip does not necessarily mean there has been a long-term decline in mental illness.

The SAMHSA report released in 2012 states that approximately 1.1 percent of adults in the United States suffer from schizophrenia, 2.6 percent of adults in the United States live with bipolar disorder, and 6.9 percent of adults in the United States—or sixteen million— had at least one major depressive episode in the past year. A further 18.1 percent of adults in the United States have experienced an anxiety disorder, such as post-traumatic stress disorder (PTSD), obsessive-compulsive disorder (OCD), and specific phobias. Among the 20.2 million adults in the United States who experienced a substance use disorder, 50.5 percent—or 10.2 million—had a cooccurring mental illness. An estimated 26 percent of homeless adults staying in shelters live with serious mental illness, and an estimated 46 percent have a severe mental illness or a substance use disorder. Approximately 20 percent of state prisoners and 21 percent of local jail prisoners have "a recent history" of a mental health condition. In the juvenile justice systems, 70 percent of youth have at least one mental health condition, and at least 20 percent live with a severe mental illness.

Each year, millions of Americans face the reality of living with the complexity of mental health conditions, as one in five US adults will experience a mental health condition in their lifetime. However, everyone is affected or impacted by mental illness through friends and family. Each year, there is a fight to try to provide support, educate the public, and advocate for equal care for mental health. Each year, the movement grows stronger and stronger. The 2018 National Mental Health Observances has a twelve-month calendar of events to help bring awareness to mental health. Check out this website: http://www.stampoutstigma. com/. Help spread the word through the many awareness, support, and advocacy activities by showing you're #IntoMentalHealth. This shows your support and helps those of us in the mental health services area provide help.

Research has documented a definite problem, a mental health problem. Now we wrestle to find a solution. Ministry, when it's with someone like you, seems relatively easy—know yourself, and you can know others. But what about those who are not like you? Not only are there personality differences among people but also brain and behavioral differences.

People struggling with complex problems hurt deeply, feel socially isolated, and are often misunderstood. What does it look like to enter into the world of someone who has been labeled with a behavioral disorder or as a social misfit or defiant? What are the unique and complex experiences of this person? Learning how to move toward those different from us with the love of Jesus will not only unite us, but it will give us a real understanding of our sameness in Christ.

Mental health helpers must have a feel for the slow processes of change, be willing to live within uncertainties, and yet keep our bearings. We must combine indestructible hope with realistic expectations. So how do we biblically and lovingly engage those who are struggling? It is my goal to help guide you through a meaningful understanding of people who have complex problems and show you how to offer biblical help.

The reality of spiritual conflict in our world is a given to those who believe the Bible, but sometimes those who are convinced of the reality of spiritual conflict deny or minimize the reality of psychological and psychiatric illness. Often, Christians suffering from mental or psychiatric illness have been treated as if they were demonized. Those who had demonic problems in addition to their psychological and psychiatric illness often get their demonic issues attended to and not their mental and psychiatric illness.

As I continue to look at this theory, I have concluded that with the fall of man, as Genesis 3 outlines, sin, death, pain, suffering, and illness came into the world. The fallen world we live in is subject to natural laws. Psychology and medicine help us deal with our problems related to natural laws. Our minds or souls contain our decision-making capacity, our desires, our will, and our emotions. The mind or soul is the realm where psychological processes take place. Our bodies, including the brain, interact with our mind and soul, and physical medicine helps us with problems related to the body, which leads me to a place of war within the self.

Spiritual warfare is the struggle against demonic forces that are trying to harm or destroy us. It is the starting place for really understanding mental illness. Without the knowledge that there really is a devil (and a multitude of demons), you will never understand what is happening to you, or why it is happening. Until you get the understanding of the devil and demons and understand that they do exist, you will never understand.

There really is a devil. The devil or Satan was created by God as an angel of enormous prestige and responsibility. The Bible tells this story: "You [Satan] were the model of perfection, full of wisdom and perfect in beauty … You were anointed as a guardian cherub, for so I [God] ordained you" (Ezekiel 28:11, 14 NIV). "You were blameless in all your ways from the day you were created till wickedness was found in you" (Ezekiel 28:15 NIV).

The Bible details how Satan fell from grace: "Your [Satan's] heart became proud on account of your beauty, and you corrupted your wisdom because of your splendor. So, I [God] threw you to the earth …" (Ezekiel 28:17 NIV). "So, I drove you in disgrace from the mount of God, and I expelled you, O guardian cherub, from among the fiery stones" (Ezekiel 28:16 NIV).

"Satan had rebelled against God. As a result, he forfeited his exalted position as a guardian cherub. And he now faces a severe future punishment as a result of his rebellion: He will be 'tormented day and night forever and ever'" (Revelation 20:10 NIV).

The devil now "leads the whole world astray" (Revelation 12:9 NIV). He is a master of deception. The devil can talk directly to God (Job 1:6). He is also "the accuser of our brothers [Christians], who accuses them before our God day and night" (Revelation 12:10 NIV). Satan was not alone in his rebellion against God. That is why there are now demons.

Satan was joined in his rebellion by one-third of the angels in heaven (Revelation 12:4). These rebellious angels were also cast out of heaven and are now on earth (Revelation 12:9). These "fallen angels" are referred to as demons.

Since there are many angels (Luke 2:13, Matthew 26:53), it stands to reason that there are many demons. These demons are under Satan's control and constitute an organized, evil spiritual army that seeks to harm or destroy every Christian (Ephesians 6:10–18). These demons can also afflict nonbelievers (Mark 5:1–20). Demonic activity can sometimes directly cause physical health problems, such as seizures (Matthew 17:14–21). However, the battleground is primarily in the mind—the central control station of the human body. Satan seeks to get us to engage in sinful thinking, which will harm us even if it does not result in sinful behavior. For example, the sin of unforgiveness is often associated with anxiety, depression, and a variety of painful physical ailments (Matthew 18:21–35). Demons can sometimes possess a nonbeliever (Mark 5:1–20). These are people over whom the demonic spirits can exert near-total control. Often, we think that only one spirit can inhabit the body. However, more than one can inhabit an individual and reside simultaneously. Demons cannot possess a believer: "He who is in you [God] is greater than he who is in the world" (1 John 4:4 NKJV). But demons can obtain spiritual footholds, which enable them to create emotional and physical distress in a variety of ways (Ephesians 4:26–27).

Paul tells us this in his letter to the church at Ephesus in Ephesians 6:10–12 (ESV), where he makes this statement:

> Finally, be strong in the Lord and in the strength of his might. Put on the whole armor of God, that you may be able to stand against the schemes of the devil. For we do not wrestle against flesh and blood, but against the rulers,

against the authorities, against the cosmic powers over this present darkness, against the spiritual forces of evil in the heavenly places.

Paul paints a picture of God's people here that is of an army. This army is committed to fight a universal war of conflict against the devil. Let's take a look at verses 10 and 11 again: "Finally, be strong in the Lord and in the strength of his might. Put on the whole armor of God, that you may be able to stand against the schemes of the devil." Paul takes for granted that we who believe that there's a God are involved in a war in which we need not bear arms. He says that we need to put on an armor so we can war against or, should I say, protect ourselves against the adversary, the devil. It is my belief that mental illness and mental disorders are connected to this war.

Now, in verse 12, it says, "For we do not wrestle against flesh and blood, but against the rulers, against the authorities, against the cosmic powers over this present darkness, against the spiritual forces of evil in the heavenly places" (ESV). This verse points out that the conflict is not against the flesh and blood of human beings but against the rulers of darkness. If we can recall, as Christians, we have come to the light so we fight to stay in the spiritual light. The forces that we fight against are the rulers' authority and powers of darkness—Satan, the devil, and his spiritual forces of evil in the heavenly world or regions.

Satan has a highly organized kingdom, believe it or not, with various levels of authority. Whether we believe it or not, Satan's kingdom is in a heavenly realm, or, should I say, his headquarters. I know that this is a shocking statement, but it is a fact. In Matthew 12:25–28 (AMP), it clearly states the fact that Satan has a kingdom (house):

> Knowing their thoughts Jesus said to them, "Any kingdom that is divided against itself is being laid waste; and no city or house divided against itself will [continue to] stand. If Satan casts out Satan [that is, his demons], he has become divided against himself and disunited; how then will his kingdom stand? If I cast out the demons by [the help of] Beelzebub (Satan), by whom do your sons drive them out? For this reason, they will be your judges. But if it is by the Spirit of God that I cast out the demons, then the kingdom of God has come upon you [before you expected it] (AMP).

Secondly, Satan's kingdom is not yet divided but highly organized, and thirdly, it stands and has not yet been overthrown. Jesus also mentions another kingdom, the kingdom of God. He brings out into the open a conflict when He said He drove out demons by the spirit of God. Then you know the kingdom of God has come.

Now, we know God's kingdom has the strongest power because an evil spirit cannot live where God dwells or resides. This gives us two kingdoms in opposition: the kingdom of God and the kingdom of Satan. We can find this to be true, for Paul wrote in Colossians 1:12–14 (ASV),

> giving thanks unto the Father, who made us meet to be partakers of the inheritance of the saints in light; who delivered us out of the power of darkness and translated us into the kingdom of the Son of his love; in whom we have our redemption, the forgiveness of our sins we see two kingdoms the Kingdom of Light and the kingdom of darkness.

The Kingdom of Light is where our inheritance lies. The Bible recognizes that Satan has some authority, whether we like it or not.

In Satan's kingdom, there are many demons, evil spirits, who serve as his servants. Based on the various records in the Bible, we can ascertain that before the six days' recovery work of the heavens and the earth, there existed a world wherein lived a group of living beings with spirits (Genesis 1 KJV):

> And the earth was without form, and void; and darkness was upon the face of the deep. And the Spirit of God moved upon the face of the waters.

> And God said, let there be light: and there was light. And God saw the light, that it was good: and God divided the light from the darkness. And God called the light Day, and the darkness he called Night. And the evening and the morning were the first day. And God said, let there be a firmament in the midst of the waters, and let it divide the waters from the waters. And God made the firmament, and divided the waters which were under the firmament from the waters which were above the firmament: and it was so. And God called the firmament Heaven. And the evening and the morning were the second day. And God said, Let the waters under the heaven be gathered together unto one place, and let the dry land appear: and it was so.

> And God called the dry land Earth; and the gathering together of the waters called he Seas: and God saw that it was good. And God said, Let the earth bring forth grass, the herb yielding seed, and the fruit tree yielding fruit after his kind, whose seed is in itself, upon the earth: and it was so. And the

earth brought forth grass, and herb yielding seed after his kind, and the tree yielding fruit, whose seed was in itself, after his kind: and God saw that it was good. And the evening and the morning were the third day. And God said, Let there be lights in the firmament of the heaven to divide the day from the night; and let them be for signs, and for seasons, and for days, and years: And let them be for lights in the firmament of the heaven to give light upon the earth: and it was so. And God made two great lights; the greater light to rule the day, and the lesser light to rule the night: he made the stars also. And God set them in the firmament of the heaven to give light upon the earth, And to rule over the day and over the night, and to divide the light from the darkness: and God saw that it was good. And the evening and the morning were the fourth day.

When Satan rebelled against God, they all followed him and rebelled together. Therefore, God judged that world, on the one hand, by shutting off the sun and moon in the sky so that they gave forth no light, and on the other hand, by destroying the earth and the living beings with water. These living beings, judged as they were by water, became separated in spirit and body. These disembodied spirits who dwell in the waters of judgment are the demons, the evil spirits mentioned in the Bible. Therefore, originally, there were three groups of characters in the kingdom of Satan: first, Satan, the head, the ruler; second, the angels who followed Satan in rebelling against God and who served as ministers and officials to rule for him in the air; third, the disembodied spirits, or the demons, the evil spirits, who acted as Satan's servants to run his errands on earth.

Later, after humans were created, Satan came to entice them and succeeded in seducing them. Humans became his kingdom's subjects, the ones he handled and abused. Therefore, there are four classes of personalities in Satan's kingdom today. In the air are Satan and his messengers, and on earth are his servants and subjects, the innumerable demons and the myriads of people. At the time when the Lord Jesus was preaching the gospel on earth, He met people everywhere who were possessed by the demons. Today, there are still flocks of demons who are maneuvering among people in this world. Although their dwelling place is in the sea, they like to seek a body where they can live. When we say a person is possessed by a demon, we usually refer to the human body being possessed by a demon.

The kingdom of Satan consists of these four classes of personalities. They are organized altogether into a system through which Satan usurps the air and the earth to the end that he may overthrow God's authority and set up his own kingdom. Therefore, this kingdom, organized by his rebellious force, is absolutely illegal. It was not until four thousand years after the fall of the human race, at the beginning of the dispensation of the New Testament, that the Lord Jesus came forth to His ministry and declared, "Repent ye: for the kingdom of heaven is at hand" (Matthew 3:2 KJV). What the Lord meant was that before this, it was the kingdom of earth, the kingdom of Satan, wherein Satan ruled, that held sway, but now it is the kingdom of heaven, the kingdom of God, coming upon this earth to reign. Later, He taught the disciples to pray, "Let thy kingdom come." The full accomplishment of this matter will be seen at the sound of the seventh trumpet in the future (Revelation 11:15). Then the kingdom of this world will become the kingdom of God and Christ. Thus, God's kingdom will practically and completely come upon the earth.

Before that day arrives, the period in which we are living is the time for the people of God to fight for Him on earth. From the time the Lord Jesus came forth to minister until the time of His second coming, all the works the people of God are doing for Him are instances of spiritual warfare. God's desire is to rescue, through those who belong to Him, the people who were captured by Satan and to recover the earth, which was usurped by Satan. This rescuing and recovering is, according to what the Lord has shown us in Matthew 12, the warfare between the kingdom of God and the kingdom of Satan.

Since warfare exists between the kingdoms of God and Satan, all the spiritual work we are doing for God, whatever form it may take, as long as it touches the things of the spiritual realm, is in nature warfare. For example, preaching the gospel, according to Acts 26:18 (ESV), is "to open their eyes, that they may turn from darkness to light and from the power of Satan unto God." This shows us the effectiveness of preaching the gospel is not only to open people's eyes and turn them from darkness to light but also to deliver them from the power of Satan. Again, Colossians 1:13 (ASV) says, "Who delivered us out of the power of darkness and translated us into the kingdom of the Son of his love." To be delivered from the power of darkness is to be delivered from the power of Satan or the kingdom of Satan. And to be translated into the kingdom of the Son of God's love is to be translated into the kingdom of God. Therefore, preaching the gospel is wholly spiritual warfare to drive out the power of Satan in people and bring in the kingdom of God.

A person who does not believe in the Lord obviously rejects the name of God, does not have God's reign in him or her, and has nothing to do with the will of God. Instead, that person is fully under the power of Satan, and his or her whole being is in the dark kingdom of Satan. When a person is saved, he or she first believes in the name of the Lord; second, he or she calls on the Lord's name; and third, he or she is in the name of the Lord—he or she belongs to the Lord's name. Hence, that person is delivered from the power of Satan and belongs to the name of the Lord. Once the name of the Lord is upon him or her, the authority of the Lord follows. Once the authority of the Lord comes upon someone, Satan's authority is removed. Therefore, strictly speaking, preaching the gospel, bringing salvation to people, and leading them to the Lord is a kind of spiritual warfare. Therefore, these two kingdoms are engaged in mortal warfare, and the war is coming to its climax in our day as this age comes to a close.

Now that I have your attention, let us find out where Satan's headquarters are located. Ephesians 6:12 states that we as Christians are in a life-and-death struggle with a highly organized kingdom inhabited by evil, rebellious spiritual beings and that the headquarters is in the heavenly realm. I know that this raises a question in most Christian minds. Satan was cast out of heaven long ago, so we wonder how he can still occupy a place in the heavenly realm. We must remember that Satan is a spirit, a disembodied spirit, and he needs a body to dwell in. That is why he gets into us and uses our bodies to work out his evil powers, causing us to be disobedient to God.

In Job 1:6 and 7 (ASV), it says,

> Now it came to pass on the day when the sons of God came to present themselves before Jehovah, that Satan also came among them. And Jehovah said unto Satan, Whence comest thou? Then Satan answered Jehovah, and said, from going to and fro in the earth, and from walking up and down in it.

These passages indicate that Satan still had access to the presence of God in heaven at that time. This is also recorded again in Job 2:1 and 2. This took place after Satan had been cast down by God. When the sons of God came to present themselves and report to God, Satan was present among them. Please note that the angels didn't recognize Satan, and we can understand why, for Paul wrote in 2 Corinthians 11:14 (KJV), "And no marvel; for Satan himself is transformed into an angel of light." *Wow*, an angel of light! Satan could appear with the other angels and not be recognized.

This is how mental illness enters, and we do not recognize it because it looks normal when it is not. It has to be exposed to the light or brought to the attention of the individual. Once it is exposed, the battle begins. You are then aware that this is a battle in the mind and that evil spiritual forces are behind it. First Corinthians 10:13 (NIV) states, "No temptation has overtaken you except what is common to mankind. And God is faithful; he will not let you be tempted beyond what you can bear. But when you are tempted, he will also provide a way out so that you can endure it." Although this scripture is speaking about sin, mental illness is not a sin. What seems to be normal overtakes a man because the thoughts become common. What seems to be clear in the mind yet has no standing against the Word of God.

Now in Revelation 12:10 (GNT), it says, "Then I heard a loud voice in heaven saying,

'Now God's salvation has come! Now God has shown his power as King! Now his Messiah has shown his authority! For the one who stood before our God and accused believers day and night has been thrown out of heaven." This verse talks about the accuser of the brethren, and, *yes*, the accuser is Satan himself. He tries to get to God before we can so that God will turn His back on us. Satan is a snitch. Satan wants the mentally ill to look unfit before God so that God would leave them to themselves and allow them to be continually tormented by the devil. In verses 11 and 12 of Revelation Chapter 12, it indicates that Satan still has access to the presence of God, and he uses his access to accuse God's people in the presence of God.

I have a question: Is there more than one heaven? Most scriptures indicate that there's more than one heaven in Genesis 1:1 in some translations. This is the first time heaven is mentioned in the Bible. Most times, it is plural. In 2 Chronicles 2:6 (NKJV), it says, "But who is able to build Him a temple, since heaven and the heaven of heavens cannot contain Him? Who am I then, that I should build Him a temple, except to burn sacrifice before Him?" This is a clear statement that there is more than one heaven and one above all the heavens.

Paul is more specific. He states that Christ was caught up into the third heaven, signifying that there is more than one. I have heard people say things about a seventh heaven, but that is not scripturally sound, if you would agree with me that the third heaven is where paradise, the place of rest of the departed righteous, is now located. This is where God Himself dwells. Ephesians 4:10 (NKJV) indicates that Jesus ascended higher than all the heavens: "He who descended is also the One who ascended far above all the heavens, that He might fill all things." Therefore, there must be at least three heavens. Can you agree that Satan's kingdom is still in a heavenly realm, but the bottomless pit, I believe, is the center of the earth or even closer to the sun? It has to be somewhere that is very hot, where the rays and the heat can burn you to a crisp.

According to the Koran, the holy book of Islam, there's a seventh heaven. The seventh heaven is a condition of happiness. The Koran is the book used by those who follow the Islamic faith. It is like their Bible. The Koran may not an appropriate book for new Christians, for they are not strong enough to discern. These theologies of the Koran can offer confusion, and God is not the author of confusion but one who gives understanding.

If you are very happy, you may feel you're on cloud nine. That is more becoming of the scriptures, for Jesus is coming back in the clouds, according to the scripture Matthew 24:30, Matthew 26:64, Mark 13:26, Mark 14:62, 1 Thessalonians 4:17, and Jude 1:12. You can read these for more clarity. Cloud nine is not established doctrine, however. If we can agree that there are at least three heavens, that fits the scriptures.

To explain, the first heaven is visible to the human eye. This is the sky, where the sun, moon, stars, and clouds reside. and we can see with our eyes the beauty of the first heaven.

The first heaven is the atmosphere, a material heaven, the physical heavens of the sky and outer space, and it has its own hosts, like birds, planets, and stars. And that's just natural. No matter how far out the Hubble Space Telescope goes and how it maps the stars, it's never going to find the real heaven of our eternity on the other side of the moon. It's just a physical reality. To make this a little clearer, the atmospheric heavens include the air that we breathe as well as the space that immediately surrounds the earth. The technical term for this is the *troposphere*. It extends about twenty miles above the earth. *Webster's* defines it as the lowest, densest part of the earth's atmosphere in which most weather changes occur and temperature generally decreases rapidly with altitude and which extends from the earth's surface to the bottom of the stratosphere at about seven miles (eleven kilometers) high. The space above this is called the "stratosphere." The celestial heaven, or the second heaven, refers to outer space or the stellar heaven. It includes the sun, moon, and stars.

The charismatic church uses the term *second heaven* in reference to Satan's domain and anything that comes from there. We take biblical descriptions of Satan being "the ruler of the kingdom of the air" (Ephesians 2:2) and demons being "the spiritual forces of evil in the heavenly realms" (Ephesians 6:12) and develop a theology of spiritual warfare. According to these beliefs, "the second heaven revelations" are false visions coming from Satan in an attempt to deceive God's prophets on earth. Prophets must learn to distinguish between "second heaven revelations" (from the devil) and "third heaven revelations" (from God). It is believed that this theology teaches a hierarchy of demonic power, with the first-heaven (earthbound) demons being of lesser authority and power than the second-heaven demons.

The third heaven is the highest of heavens, as described in Psalm 8:1 and in Ecclesiastes 5:2, for God dwells in heaven, and this is a place of paradise, the place of rest of the departed righteous. The third heaven, the one that Paul was caught up into, where he heard and saw things that could not be translated to the natural world, is that place where God Himself dwells.

> I know a man in Christ [Paul himself] who fourteen years ago, was caught up to the third heaven. Whether it was in the body or out of the body I do not know—God knows. And I know that this man—whether in the body or apart from the body I do not know, but God knows—was caught up to paradise. He heard inexpressible things, things that man is not permitted to tell. (2 Corinthians 12:1–4 BSB)

The third heaven isn't the same as the second heaven, because, remember, Lucifer, who used to be in the third heaven, was cast from heaven, and yet, everyone would acknowledge that Satan still inhabits the spiritual dimension. God cannot abide with evil, so there's no evil presence in the third heaven. Now, let's take a look at the second heaven, which I call the intermediate heaven. This must be between the first and the third heaven, and I believe this is where Satan dwells. As I have stated before, I believe this is where Satan's headquarters are located. The second heaven is what Paul calls "the heavenly places" in Ephesians 6:12, a spiritual heaven around us today, as Paul puts it: "For we are not contending against flesh and blood, but against the principalities, against the powers, against the world rulers of this present darkness, against the spiritual hosts of wickedness in the heavenly places" (Ephesians 6:12 RSV).

In this dimension of the Spirit, there are angelic forces that are godly forces, as well as demonic forces and powers.

This second heaven, spiritual atmosphere, which is cohabited by both good and evil, is a very, very small part of the cosmos. It really just surrounds this earth, the only rebellious and sinful place in the whole cosmos. This may explain why we often find ourselves in an intense wrestling match when we pray. Sometimes, we do not realize how hard it is to break through to God. We believe that God hears our prayers, but we wonder why the answer tarries. The only explanation that I have is that it involves a warfare and that satanic forces try to hold the answer from getting to us because the answer has to come through his realm in the second heaven. He holds it up there until God sends His warriors to battle and we receive the answer. Can we agree that Satan's headquarters are somewhere between the first and the third heaven, the dwelling place of God from whom all answers and blessings flow?

We look to the book of Daniel for an example of spiritual warfare. This will enlighten us about the location of Satan's headquarters, or his kingdom. We find the battle of the angels in Daniel 10. Here, in this chapter, Daniel describes the future of the people of Israel. Daniel devoted three weeks, or twenty-one days, to intensified special prayer and waiting on God for an answer for what to do for his people. At the end of the three weeks or twenty-one days of fasting and praying, an angel came from heaven with the answer to Daniel's prayer. This was a beautiful and powerful angel, and all the people with Daniel were scattered. The only one who remained to receive the Revelation from God was Daniel. The angel spoke to Daniel. We find this in Daniel 10:1–13.

We must understand the importance of the first day that Daniel began praying. That was when God dispatched or sent an angel with an answer. However, it took twenty-one days, three weeks, for the answer to arrive. This angel of the Lord was opposed by Satan and his angels, who are known as demons. Somewhere in the angel's journey from God's kingdom (heaven) to earth, the angel was required to go through Satan's kingdom in the heavenly realm. The evil fallen angel tried to prevent God's messenger angel from getting the message to Daniel. But Michael, an archangel and war angel, was dispatched to help the message to get to Daniel. We must understand that the war starts in the heavenly realm. Satan is called "the king of Persia." He's the chief ruler over Persia. Under him are various kings or lesser angels. The archangel who came to help has the title "great prince." The satanic angels were represented by their king, the prince/king of the kingdom of Persia (the supreme ruler), and under him are various subordinate rulers who had areas of authority. Each king is appointed over a group—for instance, pagan culture groups of the Persian Empire, perhaps over each pagan religious occult group.

<Insert Image : image0>

Satan has a highly organized kingdom, as you can see, with various areas in the rebellious kingdom of fallen spirit beings. We must understand that when we begin praying, it sets all heaven in motion, both the angels of God and the demons of Satan. That lets us know what prayer can do.

Satan's kingdom is not eternal. As to time, it is limited in time; as to space, it is limited to the air and the earth. Furthermore, Satan's kingdom is in darkness, the exact opposite of the kingdom of God.

In addition, there is still another great difference: God's kingdom is legal, whereas the kingdom of Satan is illegal. The whole universe was created by God and belongs to Him; hence, God has the legal right to reign. On the contrary, Satan's kingdom was established by rebellion against God; hence, it is entirely illegal. In Isaiah 14:12–15 (NKJV), it states,

> How you are fallen from heaven, O Lucifer, son of the morning! How you are cut down to the ground, you who weakened the nations! For you have said in your heart: "I will ascend into heaven, I will exalt my throne above the stars of God; I will also sit on the mount of the congregation. On the farthest sides of the north; I will ascend above the heights of the clouds, I will be like the Most High." Yet you shall be brought down to Sheol, To the lowest depths of the Pit.

The prophet Ezekiel in Ezekiel 28:11–17 (ASV) brings more light to this topic:

> Moreover the word of Jehovah came unto me, saying, Son of man, take up a lamentation over the king of Tyre, and say unto him, Thus saith the Lord Jehovah: Thou sealest up the sum, full of wisdom, and perfect in beauty. Thou wast in Eden, the garden of God; every precious stone was thy covering, the sardius, the topaz, and the diamond, the beryl, the onyx, and the jasper, the

sapphire, the emerald, and the carbuncle, and gold: the workmanship of thy tabrets and of thy pipes was in thee; in the day that thou wast created they were prepared. Thou wast the anointed cherub that covereth: and I set thee, so that thou wast upon the holy mountain of God; thou hast walked up and down in the midst of the stones of fire. Thou wast perfect in thy ways from the day that thou wast created, till unrighteousness was found in thee. By the abundance of thy traffic they filled the midst of thee with violence, and thou hast sinned: therefore, have I cast thee as profane out of the mountain of God; and I have destroyed thee, O covering cherub, from the midst of the stones of fire. Thy heart was lifted up because of thy beauty; thou hast corrupted thy wisdom by reason of thy brightness: I have cast thee to the ground; I have laid thee before kings, that they may behold thee.

Through the king of Babylon and the king of Tyre (both of whom had been instruments utilized by Satan), God relates the process of Satan's rebellion. Satan was originally an anointed cherub, the archangel, who occupied a special place before God. Since he was proud in heart and desired to exalt himself to equality with God, he rebelled against God and tried to overthrow God's authority, thereby establishing his own authority. Since then, there has existed in the universe the illegal kingdom of Satan.

Satan's kingdom is the sphere of Satan's reign. The Lord Jesus once called Satan "the prince of the world" (John 14:30 (AMP): "I will not speak with you much longer, for the ruler of the world (Satan) is coming. And he has no claim on Me [no power over Me nor anything that he can use against Me]"). This reveals that Satan not only has his kingdom but also reigns in his kingdom. Moreover, within his kingdom are his messengers of various ranks, all of whom were angels who followed Satan in rebelling against God. Today, these are the principalities, powers, rulers, dominions, and spiritual hosts of wickedness of the air, Satan being their head (Ephesians 6:12, 2:2, 1:21).

As we look closer at Satan's kingdom, we can see there are many demons, evil spirits, who serve as his servants. Based on the various records in the Bible, we can ascertain that before the six days' recovery work of the heavens and the earth (Genesis 1), there existed a world wherein there was a group of living beings with spirits. When Satan rebelled against God, they all followed him and rebelled together. Therefore, God judged that world, on one hand by shutting off the sun and moon in the sky so that they gave forth no light and on the other hand by destroying the earth and the living beings with water. These living beings, judged as they were by water, became separated in spirit and body. These disembodied spirits who dwell in the waters of judgment are the demons, the evil spirits, mentioned in the Bible.

Therefore, originally, there were three groups of characters in the kingdom of Satan: first, Satan, the head, the ruler; second, the angels who followed Satan in rebelling against God and who served as ministers and officials to rule for him in the air; and third, the disembodied spirits, or the demons, the evil spirits, who acted as Satan's servants to run his errands on earth.

Later, after humans were created, Satan came to entice them and succeeded in seducing them. Humans became his kingdom's subjects, the ones he handled and abused. Therefore, there are four classes of personalities in Satan's kingdom today. In the air are Satan and his messengers, and on earth are his servants and subjects, the innumerable demons and the myriads of people. At the time when the Lord Jesus was preaching the gospel on earth, He met people everywhere who were possessed by the demons. Today, there are still flocks of demons who are maneuvering among people in this world. Although their dwelling place is in the sea, they like to seek a body where they can live. When we say a person is possessed by a demon, we usually refer to the human body being possessed by a demon. Remember that Satan and his host are disembodied spirits that need a host to dwell in. Christians cannot be possessed by demons; however, they are tormented with thoughts, and this torment is the open door of mental illness.

What I visualize is the kingdom of Satan consists of these four classes of personalities. They are organized altogether into a system through which Satan usurps the air and the earth to the end that he may overthrow God's authority and set up his own kingdom. Therefore, this kingdom, organized by Satan's rebellious force, is absolutely illegal. It was not until four thousand years after the fall of the human race, at the beginning of the dispensation of the New Testament, that the Lord Jesus came forth to His ministry and declared, "Repent ye: for the kingdom of heaven is at hand." What the Lord meant was that before this, it was the kingdom of earth, the kingdom of Satan, wherein Satan ruled, that held sway, but now it is the kingdom of heaven, the kingdom of God, coming upon this earth to reign. Later, He taught the disciples to pray, "Let thy kingdom come." The full accomplishment of this matter will be seen at the sound of the seventh trumpet in the future (Revelation 11:15). Then the kingdom of this world will become the kingdom of God and Christ. Thus, God's kingdom will practically and completely come upon the earth.

I'll start with this scripture: "Be self-controlled and alert. Your enemy the Devil prowls around like a roaring lion looking for someone to devour" (1 Peter 5:8 NIV). The devil is the adversary of every Christian. The battleground is primarily in your mind. Satan will try to hurt you in any way he can. However, his power is limited; he can only do what God allows (e.g., Job 1:1–12). Here are some common things that the devil does: He may put disturbing, discouraging, and destructive thoughts into your mind (examples, *It's hopeless!*

You're a loser. I want to kill myself. I want to get high. No one cares whether I live or die. The world will be a better place without me).

Satan can put evil, violent, gross, perverted, jealous, critical, or foolish thoughts into your mind. He can seek to get you to dwell on an unpleasant event such that you become angry, worried, or depressed. Sometimes these thoughts involve the distortion or misapplication of scripture. Satan can and does pretend to be the voice of God. Satan can also sometimes influence others so that they create problems for you. Then there's what psychologists refer to as auditory/visual/tactile hallucinations: Some people hear voices, see corresponding visions of someone talking to them, or feel bodily sensations that are without physical explanation (e.g., "I get raped every night"). In my estimation, most of these "hallucinations" are, in fact, demonic.

Also, anytime you find yourself doing something to hurt yourself or others, it is likely that demonic forces are involved—especially in these two ways: 1) You are hurting yourself to relieve emotional pain caused by a satanic foothold (e.g., cutting to relieve the emotional pain associated with having been sexually abused), and 2) you are harming others—especially involuntarily—as a result of demonic pressure (e.g., involuntarily making disrespectful comments about others as part of your Tourette's disorder).

Here are some things the Bible says about Satan. He is a deceiver (1 Timothy 4:1–3, Colossians 2:8). He seeks to distort or misapply scripture for his own purposes (Matthew 4:1–11). He is a liar and murderer (John 8:44). He encourages child abuse—to the extent of murder (Psalm 106:37). He is the spiritual author of false religions (2 Corinthians 11:1–15). He seeks to impede believers in their endeavors (1 Thessalonians 2:18). He tempts us to sin (Genesis 3). He encourages envy and selfish ambition (James 3:14). He torments with mental illness (Mark 5:120). Second Corinthians 10:3–5 (NIV) says,

> For though we live in the world, we do not wage war as the world does. The weapons we fight with are not the weapons of the world. On the contrary, they have divine power to demolish strongholds. We demolish arguments and every pretension that sets itself up against the knowledge of God, and we take captive every thought to make it obedient to Christ.

Mental health can be considered as a stronghold. Strongholds can be a source of protection for us from the devil, as is the case when the Lord becomes our stronghold, as He did for David. However, a stronghold can also be a source of defense for the devil's influence in our lives, where demonic or sinful activity is actually defended within our sympathetic thoughts toward evil. I'm not implying that all mental illness is demonic and to be cast out with prayer and exorcism, as was believed in days of old. However, some mental illnesses are, and they are forces that we deal with in our clients and counselees. Mental illness is a chemical imbalance within the human brain.

Mental health includes our emotional, psychological, and social well-being. It affects how we think, feel, and act. It also helps determine how we handle stress, relate to others, and make choices. Mental health is important at every stage of life, from childhood and adolescence through adulthood. I believe you are getting the picture that I have painted for you.

Graham C. L. Davey, PhD, is a professor of psychology at the University of Sussex, United Kingdom. His research interests extend across mental health problems generally and anxiety and worry specifically. Professor Davey has published over 140 articles in scientific and professional journals and written or edited sixteen books, including *Psychopathology*, *Clinical Psychology*, *Applied Psychology*, *Complete Psychology*, *Worrying and Psychological Disorders*, and *Phobias: A Handbook of Theory, Research, and Treatment*. He has served as president of the British Psychological Society and is currently editor in chief of the *Journal of Experimental Psychopathology*. Dr. Davey wrote an article posted December 31, 2014, in *Psychology Today* titled "Spirit Possession and Mental Health." I found this article very interesting. He writes,

> Even today, many cultures still believe that unusual behavior that may be symptomatic of mental health problems is caused by spirit possession especially in some less developed areas of the world where such beliefs are still important features of the local culture. Interestingly, beliefs about spirit possession are not simply used to try and explain the effects of psychopathology-related experiences but are also regularly used to control and coerce individuals.

He goes further to say that in 2012, a study by Neuner, Pfeiffer, Schauer-Kaiser, and Odenwald et alia investigated the theory of a variant of spirit possession in youths aged between twelve and twenty-five years in war-affected regions of Northern Uganda. They compared youths who had been abducted and forced to fight as child soldiers in the so-called **Lord**'s Resistance Army, a group that had waged a long and brutal campaign to overthrow the government of Uganda, and youths who had never been abducted. In the conclusion, they found that culturally this is believed to be true, and Dr. Davey also concurs with the findings.

There have been many articles and papers written on research on mental illness linking it to supernatural beliefs. One writer concludes, "Supernatural beliefs are common in patients with schizophrenia and many of them attribute the symptoms of mental disorders to these beliefs." (East Asian Psychiatry.2014 June 24)

Satanic Umbrella Chart

SATAN MENTAL ILLNESS CHART BREAKDOWN

Each tip/rib of the diagram above is a representation of Satan's kingdom, taking place in the mind of the individual or client. Because Satan has a highly organized kingdom with various levels of authority, in the preceding diagram is the vision of how I believe Satan works in the mind of the counselee. Our client will be able to overcome these, but it will take time. We take a preview of the *Diagnostic and Statistical Manual of Mental Disorders 5* edition. I take a look at each section. This is the course by which I seek to show the spiritual battle in the mind of the individual or client.

The top of the umbrella in the center is Satan. Under him, he has demons under the demons, he has emps or spiritual little forces that are sent to torment humanity. Let me be clear that each rib of the umbrella is connected to the top, and from the top, everything moves to the tip of the rib.

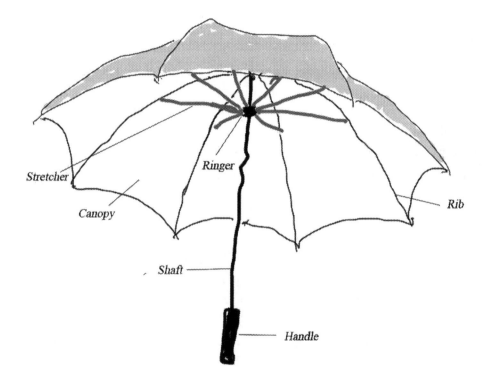

Malik Sealy

The Shaft = Satan
The Rib = Demons
The Tip = Imps (small, mischievous devils or sprites)
The Runner = The Spiritual Forces

Merrill Unger, a former professor at Dallas Theological Seminary best known for writing *Unger's Bible Handbook,* in his book *Biblical Demonology: A Study of Spiritual Forces at*

Work Today, presents a scriptural view of "demonization" based upon a natural and literal interpretation of the inerrant scripture. This is the definition to which this work adheres.

When viewing the biblical narratives of encounters with demonized people, it is clear that an actual state of inhabitation and control by one or more demons occurs. These demons are individuals by nature. Unger then distinguishes between ordinary temptations and assaults of Satan and demonization. With ordinary assaults of Satan, the human will consciously yields to the will of Satan and gradually assumes the characteristics of a satanic nature. Demonization, however, accelerates this process and will result in an almost complete deprivation of reason or ability to choose such that a twofold consciousness is produced within a person. This state of almost complete loss of control may have arisen because of the continual consent of the demonized to sin.

In modern days, an increased interest in spiritual warfare has occurred because of the rise of beliefs such as those in the Charismatic Movement and Pentecostal denominations that emphasize a personal experience with God. Spiritual warfare includes understanding the authority of Jesus Christ along with the subject of delivering a person from the presence of a demon, also known as "demonization." There are two predominant approaches to directly confronting the demonic in an effort to bring spiritual freedom to a demonized individual: the "truth encounter" and the "power encounter."

The "power encounter" evokes the name of Jesus Christ while directly confronting a demon and commanding it to leave, as seen practiced in the New Testament narratives about Jesus and His disciples. The power encounter usually involves the verification of faith in Christ and includes forgiveness and repentance of sin, as well as some of the steps that occur in "truth encounters." The actual power encounter involves, at a minimum, the discernment of the presence of a demon within a person and the forceful eviction of it by commanding it to leave.

In the mind of the counselee, we have to remember that once we discern we have to take steps from a perspective of deliverance and healing, as I will explain throughout this work, that the cause is not clear to the science of mental health. I do believe that it all has to start from the beginning, and it raises its head as an individual grows. I take a look at some of these disorders and see how the demonic forces are the direct cause of them.

Chapter 2

RIB 1: NEURODEVELOPMENTAL DISORDERS

The neurodevelopmental disorders are groups of conditions with onset in the development period. Satan causes this to manifest during the early development periods, often during childhood before the child enters preschool. We will call these developmental deficits that produce impairments of personal, social, academic, or occupational functioning. Taking a closer look, we see this is a growth impairment that develops in the brain and central nervous system. This is a disorder of the brain affecting emotion, learning ability, self-control, and memory and develops and unfolds as the individual develops and grows. This demonic force grabs hold of the mind at a young age when it goes unnoticed and sets up strategies from specific limitations of learning or control of executive functions to global impairments of social skills or intelligence. The imps #1 from tip #1 spring autism spectrum disorder (see following diagram). This demonic force sends the imp to confuse genetics and environmental factors. The signs appear between ages two and three. Some cases are diagnosed as early as eighteen months.

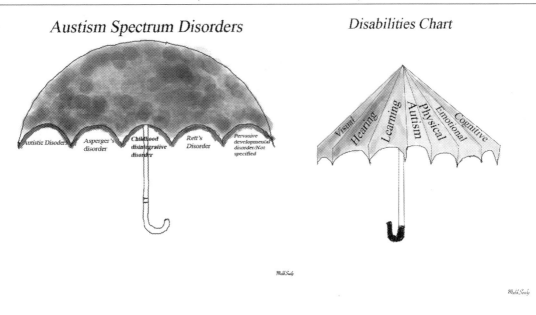

Austism Spectrum Disorders

Disabilities Chart

You can see by the umbrella of autism that it is an organized kingdom with many moving components. This imp, under the neurodevelopment demon, breaks down into smaller imps and causes problems in vision, hearing, learning, and physical, emotional, and cognitive areas. Autism is no accident of nature. It is a real affectation of consciousness due to environmental and subtle energy forces that affect the ability of consciousness in autistic children to perform in what we consider "normal" ways.

William Stillman has reached way out of the box by asking the reader to consider that there are other possibilities in play regarding the direction of humanity. There seems not to be a cure-all for this disorder. With my research, I found that an Epsom salt bath will calm the child. Epsom salt has magnesium. When the body absorbs this, the child will be easier to get to sleep. The sulfur supports detoxification, just about one cup per bath.

There are essential fatty acids that are able to reduce aggression and support a healthy immune system. Essential fatty acids are major components of the brain cells. Fish oil capsules are high in DHA.

The gospel accounts are filled with numerous stories of sicknesses being miraculously healed by Jesus Christ. Two thousand years ago, people had different explanations and understanding of the diseases and disorders we see today. In Mark 9, we read a story of Jesus healing a young boy. This boy is often described as having been healed of epilepsy because he had a seizure right before Jesus healed him, but the boy's affliction was more than epilepsy. The boy in this story suffered from what doctors today call autism. Autism is a group of developmental brain disorders, collectively called autism spectrum disorder (ASD).

The term *spectrum* refers to the wide range of symptoms, skills, and levels of impairment, or disability, that children with ASD can have. Some children are mildly impaired by their symptoms, but others are severely disabled. While the story of the healing of this boy is found in three of the four gospels, I will use the account in the gospel of Mark to support my school of thought.

Mark 9:17—29 (NKJV) reads,

> Then one of the crowd answered and said, "Teacher, I brought You my son, who has a mute spirit. And wherever it seizes him, it throws him down; he foams at the mouth, gnashes his teeth, and becomes rigid. So, I spoke to Your disciples, that they should cast it out, but they could not." He answered him and said, "O faithless generation, how long shall I be with you? How long shall I bear with you? Bring him to Me." Then they brought him to Him. And when he saw Him, immediately the spirit convulsed him, and he fell on the ground and wallowed, foaming at the mouth.

The child afflicted with the spirit is a boy. Autism is four to five times more common in boys than girls. An estimated 1 out 54 boys and 1 in 252 girls are diagnosed with autism in the United States. The father also describes a mute spirit, meaning that his son was unable to talk. About 25 percent of individuals with ASD are nonverbal. This would have been referred to as having a mute spirit in Jesus's time. In verse 18, the father also explains that the boy has seizures, and today, it is estimated that as many as one-third of individuals with ASD also have epilepsy. The father attributes the cause of the seizures to the mute spirit.

Mark 9:21–22 (NKJV) says, "So He asked his father, 'How long has this been happening to him?' And he said, 'From childhood. And often he has thrown him both into the fire and into the water to destroy him. But if You can do anything, have compassion on us and help us.'"

Because the father understands that a spirit causes his son's behavior, he describes the spirit as "throwing" his son into fire and water on different occasions to try to kill him. Today, children with autism are known to "wander, bolt, or elope" to unsafe areas like water and traffic. About half of children with ASD wander from safe to unsafe environments and about one-third of children with autism who wander are nonverbal, just like the boy in the story.

In 2012, the National Autism Association found that from 2009 to 2011, accidental drowning accounted for 91 percent of total US deaths reported in children with autism subsequent to wandering. This is actually the same type of spirit that the boy had thousands of years ago throwing these children into the water to destroy them. The father attributes all these symptoms to a mute spirit that has been afflicting the boy since childhood, and because the child is still a boy, childhood would indicate early childhood, when autism becomes evident in individuals.

Many children with autism can even begin to develop language skills and then suddenly lose them and stop speaking. The young boy in the story is a nonverbal child with autism who also suffers from frequent seizures and elopement. His level of autism on the spectrum would be considered severe.

Mark 9:23–27 (NKJV) says,

> Jesus said to him, "If you can believe, all things are possible to him who believes." Immediately the father of the child cried out and said with tears, "Lord, I believe; help my unbelief!" When Jesus saw that the people came running together, He rebuked the unclean spirit, saying to it: "Deaf and dumb spirit, I command you, come out of him and enter him no more!" Then the spirit cried out, convulsed him greatly, and came out of him. And he became as one dead, so that many said, "He is dead." But Jesus took him by the hand and lifted him up, and he arose.

This behavior was not caused by any medical or biological reason as doctors today report. It was caused by a foreign entity, which was in the child, carrying out these behaviors that characterize autism. Jesus simply commanded the spirit to leave the boy, and it did. I also want to point out that Jesus referred to this spirit as a "deaf and dumb" spirit. As mentioned earlier, the boy did not speak, like many children with autism. This accounts for the spirit being characterized as dumb, but many children with autism also do not respond to their names or when people speak to them. This is why Jesus characterizes the spirit as being a deaf spirit as well. Though there is no medical problem that impacts hearing, the spirit causes them to behave as though they are deaf.

Mark 9:28–29 (NKJV) reads, "And when He had come into the house, His disciples asked Him privately, 'Why could we not cast it out?' So He said to them, 'This kind can come out by nothing but prayer and fasting.'"

Jesus's disciples were able to cast out other spirits in the same manner that Jesus did, but they could not cast out this deaf and dumb spirit from the young boy. Jesus said it was because this particular spirit only comes out by prayer and fasting. This is the permanent cure for autism. Jesus's disciples did not fast, and that was why they could not cast it out?

I can prove this through the scripture in Luke 5:33–35 (NKJV), when Jesus is questioned about His disciples not fasting.

> Then they said to Him, "Why do the disciples of John fast often and make prayers, and likewise those of the Pharisees, but Yours eat and drink?" And He said to them, "Can you make the friends of the bridegroom fast while the bridegroom is with them? But the days will come when the bridegroom will be taken away from them; then they will fast in those days."

For me, it is very clear that what we call autism today is what was referred to as a deaf and dumb spirit in this scripture account. As far as I know, children who are given this diagnosis live with the effects of this spirit for the rest of their lives. *God did not create anyone with autism.* A demonic spirit causes autism, and it can only be removed by prayer and fasting. God can do all things with our faith, for without faith, it is impossible to please God. Yet it may take *now faith*, not yesterday's faith.

The diagnosis of autism falls on a spectrum and afflicts each individual in different ways. No matter the symptoms being displayed, it can be completely healed. No one has to live with this affliction for the rest of his or her life. If this is hard for you to accept in your spirit, call out to the Lord in the same way the boy's father did and say, "Help my unbelief!" (Mark 9:24).

The imp #2 from the first tip is called attention-deficit/hyperactivity disorder (ADHD) here. This child also has a specific learning disorder. Here, the child or individual has a persistent pattern of inattention and or hyperactive and impulsive behavior that interferes with functioning or development. This imp of inattention causes you to look for six or more symptoms found in the *DSM-5*. You will notice that this will be over a period of six months. You may notice, to some degree, inconsistencies during the child development stages. Let me take some time and explain inattention in layman's terms. It's a simple failure to pay attention to something, and it goes unnoticed for a long period of time. In psychology, it's the inability to direct and sustain attention. Direct attention refers to the ability to select relevant information to pay attention to while ignoring information that is nonrelevant. For example, your focus should have been on the basketball (relevant information) while you were playing; however, you were distracted by the beautiful butterflies (nonrelevant information) and missed the pass.

Sustained attention refers to the ability to focus on something for an extended amount of time—that is, for the amount of time it takes you to complete the task or absorb all of the relevant information. In the preceding example, you could not pay attention long enough to complete the basketball game, so you left before the game was over.

It is easier for individuals with ADHD to sustain and direct attention while they are doing something enjoyable. Think about the preceding example. As long as the basketball is in your hand, you pay enough attention to dribble it and make shots. It is when the ball leaves your hand that you have trouble sustaining attention.

You may notice negative impacts directly on social and academic or occupational actives. This individual seems to be defiant or hostile or just to fail to understand some instructions or a task. These individuals often fail to give close attention to detail or make careless mistakes in schoolwork, at work, or during activities. Children and adults will have difficulties sustaining attention in task or play activities, and the list goes on.

ADD/ADHD is an epidemic in our country. The only apparent remedy is medical intervention with drugs similar to Ritalin. Since the chemical formula for Ritalin mimics the chemical formula for cocaine, is it any wonder that the results we are expecting, normally acting and behaving children, eventually disappear? The problem is worse than we think because now ADD/ADHD is no longer confined to children, as people in their forties are now claiming they have the condition.

Those in the Christian community have largely accepted the medical opinion, and as a result, I believe many of our children that we are trying to nurture in the Lord are growing up medicated simply because parents have lost the ability and perhaps even the desire to control their behavior. Something seems to have gone haywire with our faith because, in the case of these medical conditions, Christians appear to trust the medication more than the Master Healer, who said at least six times in scripture, "I am the God that healeth thee."

The reason God appointed mothers and fathers to provide loving care and guidance for their children is that He intended for mothers and fathers to call their children's spirits to life. For those unfamiliar with the term "calling the spirit to life," let me briefly explain. We are created by the Heavenly Father as beings in His image, spirit, soul, and body. When God breathed into Adam, He blew into man the spirit portion of his existence, and it is the spirit that gives man life and makes man "the image of God." God is a spiritual being, and He has imparted to man the spirit. Since God is a Spirit, all life in the universe comes from the foundation of the spirit and spiritual principles.

In the body-soul-spirit model of the function of man, it is the spirit that is supposed to be alive and in charge of man. Specifically, it is the spirit that is *supposed* to be in charge of the soul (or our mind, will, and emotions). It is also the spirit that is supposed to be in charge of our bodies. If a person's personal spirit has not been "called to life," then the mind, will, emotions, and body will rule over man's existence. If the spirit is not in control, then the person will ultimately reflect the results of a different operation than the one God intended. The results are disastrous.

In the case of those with ADD/ADHD, the physical symptoms are obvious. Adults and children act as if they have no control. Their emotions are volatile (sometimes bipolar disorder develops from the mood swings); they cannot fully concentrate on any one thing for very long because their mind runs constantly and changes focus almost at random times to random subjects; their bodies are restless, meaning they always have to be active. The physical lack of ability to sit still is probably the most observable trait because a child cannot sit still for any more than a couple of minutes at a time. Even under correction, the need to move is so pervasive that the child will risk severe discipline in order to satisfy the need to be in motion. There are times when I discipline my grandson. I will say to him, "Sit still, and don't move." It is so difficult for him to sit still for more than two minutes. Soon, he is moving his hands, scratching his nose, or touching parts of his body (e.g., face, neck, head). The overall result of this is a frenetic individual who appears to have no sense of control and no ability to explain why he cannot control his behavior or his emotions.

From outward evaluation, these individuals seem to be oblivious to their behavior, and their responses to questioning are unsatisfactory. They are labelled with "an attitude problem." Gradually, this label sticks and becomes an excuse for why they are the way they are.

Because their spirit has not been called fully to life, they have no internal "governor" (or controller) that provides them with internal signals to adjust their emotions, to shut down streams of thought that won't stop, that allows them to sit and rest peacefully, and that allows them to be sentient beings that are aware of how their behavior influences others. When the spirit is fully alive, it adjusts the function of the brain to learn acceptable behavior. A living personal spirit allows for a variety of emotions as God intended and also allows the individual to learn what expressions are acceptable under what conditions. It also allows an active person to be able to rest, free of physical activity so that other functions (such as learning in school) can take place. The living personal spirit allows the development of intellect where an individual learns from mistakes without the need for repeating that mistake many times before learning the lesson. The living personal spirit also integrates the complete function of spirit, soul, and body into an interactive and balanced human being capable of manners, respect, stability, and adult functioning without assistance.

We are in a current state of existence in our society where we have lost at least two generations to the ADD/ADHD condition because parents, especially Christian parents, did not know to call their children's spirits to life, nor did they know how to do so. As a result, we have at least one generation of parents whose spirits have not been called to life, nor have their children's. And we wonder why our society is "on a course for disaster." It is our own fault. But God is giving us a chance to begin now. All is *not* lost, for if we begin to call our children's spirits to life, they can begin to call their children's spirits to life, and we can begin to call a *giant* generational blessing into existence—the creation of a nation of people whose spirits are living and active and calling upon the name of the Lord.

There are numerous biological theories that attempt to explain ADD or ADHD, but as of this date, there are no medical tests to detect its existence. Many in the biblical and Christian counseling arena believe that ADHD is a spiritual problem. In a recently released book by Dr. David Tyler and Dr. Kurt Grady titled, *ADHD: Deceptive Diagnosis*, they claim that a child's lack of self-discipline, self-control, and self-motivation, their disobedience, and their bad attitudes are excused as a disease.

Both the physical and spiritual areas must be taken seriously. If one believes that ADD or ADHD is a spiritual problem, one can't ignore the spiritual aspects of ADHD (that is, repentance, faith, and obedience). Also, if you ignore the physical or cerebral-related strengths and weaknesses, the child will become frustrated because of your unrealistic expectations.

Physical problems, strengths, and weaknesses obviously influence behavior. In a child labeled ADHD, the physical strengths could, since no one is born with wisdom; you have hope in prescribing a lifelong pursuit of biblical wisdom. We often think that ADHD is an unchangeable genetic malady. However, when viewed through the lens of wisdom, we can have confidence that change is possible because God gives wisdom to those who seek it. Some thoughts on how to teach wisdom: you don't have to teach everything all at once. Work on one principle at a time, and make sure you include yourself as a teachable student. Become an expert in the book of Proverbs, and emphasize encouragement and instruction more than punishment.

Does popular secular literature have anything profitable to say about how to deal with ADHD? Yes, it does. Here are a few tips: Be on the lookout for and encourage strengths. Offer instruction in a vivid, visual, concrete, and memorable way. Instead of saying, "Clean your room," say, "Put all the books on this shelf." Provide structure by way of boundaries, guidelines, reminders, and limits. Have predictable, clear, simple, and written household rules. Anticipate and preempt problems rather than react to them. Develop "to-do" lists with reasonable deadlines, and do the hard task before the easy one.

Parenting a child with ADHD is similar to parenting any other child—that is, you tailor your biblical instructions to the child's abilities. ADHD children have God-given strengths and will take more careful observation and some creative teaching. They will pose unique parenting challenges. Instead of trusting in our own strategies and natural skills, we need to also rely on the insights of the Holy Spirit.

Include a high energy level, creativity, risk taking, and an extroverted personality. Physical problems could be poor memory, difficulties with cognitive problem solving, an inability to establish priorities, and so on.

Our spiritual essence is frequently discarded when discussing ADHD. By spiritual, I mean that humans are creatures of God who live before Him in all aspects of our lives. We constantly make choices as to whether we will trust God or submit to our own desires. Spiritual problems can be identified by determining if the particular behavior violates God's law. If it does, then the behavior can be classified as a spiritual problem.

Our spiritual essence is frequently discarded when discussing ADHD. By spiritual, I mean that humans are creatures of God who live before Him in all aspects of our lives. We constantly make choices as to whether we will trust God or submit to our own desires. Spiritual problems can be identified by determining if the particular behavior violates God's law. If it does, then the behavior can be classified as a spiritual problem.

Although the Bible clearly states that children are to obey their parents, what if the child did not understand or remember the instruction? Lack of understanding or forgetfulness may not be a sin unto itself. Parents should ensure that they have given instructions that are clearly understood. Parents need to be attentive when their children disobey their commands and rules.

The *DSM-4* provides a good description of the behavior but does not offer an explanation. The lists are helpful, as they focus our attention on certain behaviors. Unfortunately, they imply that the problem has to do with a genetic disorder when it actually is character.

Biblically speaking, it is important to recognize that ADD and ADHD have spiritual implications. The Bible speaks to many of the behavioral symptoms associated with ADD and ADHD. Understanding that ADD and ADHD are lifelong medical conditions and knowing some of the ways the conditions can be treated help us better equip those with ADD and ADHD to follow godly standards. Also, knowing that the hope of the gospel and the truth that God are transforming each of us gives us grace for those suffering from ADD and ADHD. No one lives a godly life easily. Recognizing our limitations—be they the general limitation of a sinful nature or a medical limitation that affects our brain or an emotional wound that affects our ability to relate—helps us be more aware of our weaknesses and more attuned to the ways in which God can show Himself strong in that area. Second Corinthians 12:9–10 (NIV) says,

But he said to me, "My grace is sufficient for you, for my power is made perfect in weakness." Therefore, I will boast all the more gladly of my weaknesses, so that the power of Christ may rest upon me. For the sake of Christ, then, I am content with weaknesses, insults, hardships, persecutions, and calamities. For when I am weak, then I am strong.

With that in mind, let's look at what the Bible says about the behaviors associated with ADD and ADHD. The following are biblical teachings concerning the issue of attentiveness.

Equipping individuals with ADD and ADHD to live a godly life involves many factors. Certainly, those who suffer from ADD or ADHD should seek the advice of a medical professional experienced in managing ADD/ADHD. And parents, pastors, and all who work with children and adults with ADD or ADHD should also utilize the Word of God, which is profitable for teaching, reproving, correcting, and instructing. Second Timothy 3:16 (ESV) says, "All Scripture is breathed out by God and profitable for teaching, for reproof, for correction, and for training in righteousness, that the man of God may be complete, equipped for every good work."

Chapter 3

RIBS 2 AND 3: SCHIZOPHRENIA SPECTRUM AND OTHER PSYCHOTIC DISORDERS

Schizophrenia spectrum and other psychotic disorders and schizotypal personality disorder, as found in the *DSM-5* (2013), are defined by abnormalities in one in one or more of these five domains, or, as I will call them, imps of the demon of schizophrenia:

- Imp# 1—delusion
- Imp# 2—hallucination
- Imp # 3—disorganized thinking (speech)
- Imp # 4—gross disorganized or abnormal motor behavior
- Imp# 5—negative symptoms.

Schizophrenia is a long-term mental disorder. This imp is powerful, overtaking your thoughts, emotions, and behavior; causing faulty perception, inappropriate actions and feelings, and withdrawal from reality; and taking the individuals' mind into fantasy and delusion.

The National Institute of Mental Health describe schizophrenia as a chronic and severe mental disorder that affects how a person thinks, feels, and behaves. People with schizophrenia may seem like they have lost touch with reality. Although schizophrenia is not as common as other mental disorders, the symptoms can be very disabling. Symptoms of schizophrenia usually start between ages sixteen and thirty. In rare cases, children have schizophrenia too.

Schizophrenia has become one of the leading types of mental disease. It literally means "splitting of the mind," or "split personality." Schizophrenia is characterized by retreating from reality, indifference, withdrawal, hallucinations, and delusions of persecution and omnipotence, often with unimpaired intelligence.

False perceptions, or hallucinations, can appear in the form of sounds. The schizoid person may "hear" voices and believe in their reality or even "see" things that the normal person cannot see.

False beliefs, or delusions, are another symptom of this disorder. There is a distortion of the usual logical relations between ideas and a separation between the intellect and emotions so that the afflicted person exhibits irrational behavior that is not appropriate to the circumstance. There is a reduced tolerance to social intercourse and thus a retreat into a fantasy world of delusions and hallucinations. The fantasy life or eccentric behavior is sometimes characterized by nomadism or by religiosity.

Although it is not a popular belief, we understand through the New Testament that many mental diseases are precipitated by demonic influences. Psychologists do not know the cause of schizophrenia and thus cannot attack the malady directly. Their methods of shock therapy, drug therapy, and psychosurgery have varying results. Many "experts" believe that relations with the family, especially with the mother during early life, play an important role in the development of schizophrenia. A warm, understanding relationship in the family, they believe, is the best prevention for this disorder. As we shall see, this is an accurate observation.

The symptoms of schizophrenia fall into three categories: positive, negative, and cognitive.

POSITIVE SYMPTOMS

Positive symptoms are psychotic behaviors not generally seen in healthy people. People with positive symptoms may "lose touch" with some aspects of reality. The imp symptoms include the following:

- hallucinations
- delusions
- thought disorders (unusual or dysfunctional ways of thinking)
- movement disorders (agitated body movements)

NEGATIVE SYMPTOMS

Negative symptoms are associated with disruptions to normal emotions and behaviors. The imp symptoms include the following:

- flat affect (reduced expression of emotions via facial expression or voice tone)
- reduced feelings of pleasure in everyday life
- difficulty beginning and sustaining activities
- reduced speaking

COGNITIVE SYMPTOMS

For some patients, the cognitive symptoms of schizophrenia are subtle, but for others, they are more severe, and patients may notice changes in their memory or other aspects of thinking. The imp symptoms include the following:

- poor executive functioning (the ability to understand information and use it to make decisions)
- trouble focusing or paying attention
- problems with working memory (the ability to use information immediately after learning it)

How does a counselor in the Christian tradition begin to handle the many problems of schizophrenic behavior? That a person experiencing such problems may be subject to (or may subject him- or herself to) internal and external forces that may impair his or her ability to function, that he or she is capable of intentionally and unintentionally stimulating and simulating such impairment in order to mislead, and that over a period of time (or suddenly), he or she can develop such faulty responses to stress situations that he or she loses his or her grip on reality (that is, may misread it) is to picture him or her at once as a frail, conniving, self-deceptive, and foolish being. That is to say, as Christians look at it, the person is a sinner, who, according to the Bible, has been subjected by God to vanity because of his or her rebellion against his or her Creator.

Sin, the violation of God's laws, has both direct and indirect consequences that account for all of the bizarre behavior of schizophrenics. That is why Christians must refuse to ignore the biblical data. From the perspective of these Scriptural data, all faulty behavior (which for the Christian is behavior that does not conform to the law of God) stems ultimately from the fundamental impairment of each human being at birth in consequence of the corruption of mankind resulting from the fall. No perfect human beings are born by ordinary generation. They all inherit the fallen nature of Adam together with its organic and moral defects that lead to all faulty (including all bizarre) behavior. No aspect of a human being, no function, has escaped the distorting effects of sin. To some extent, therefore, the same problems seen in schizophrenics are common to all. The differences lie in (1) what bodily functions are impaired, (2) how severely, and (3) what sinful life responses have been developed by the counselee. It is also vital to ask whether the individual is redeemed by the grace of God, since redemption involves a gradual renewal of human nature (Ephesians 4:22–24; Colossians 3:10).

The identification of the problem of schizophrenia as a theological difficulty points toward a theological solution. In the same way, a nontheological diagnosis ("mental illness," and so on) leads to a nontheological solution. Wrong labels point in wrong directions, which, in turn, end only in more frustration. Schizophrenia is a psychological or psychiatric label that leads toward psychological or psychiatric solutions. If, however, investigation shows that a particular kind of bizarre behavior should be labeled as a chemical malfunction (stemming not from personal sin, such as sleep loss, but is rather solely the result of the fall), that conclusion leads toward a medical solution. If it indicates that the problem comes from sinful living, the term *sin* points in the direction of a theological solution. It is a serious fault thus to suggest that anything less than God Himself can solve a problem that fundamentally has to do with one's relationship to Him.

The Christian counselor's approach, therefore, will begin with an attempt to discover whether the behavior of any given counselee stems fundamentally from organic defects or from sinful behavior on his or her part. In the case of bizarre behavior, whenever indicated, he or she will insist upon careful medical examinations to detect any glandular or other chemical malfunction, brain damage, toxic problems, and so on. But when he or she is reasonably assured that (at base) the problem is not organic (or that it is not only organic), he or she will counsel on the supposition that such behavior must stem from sinful life patterns. The counselor will be aware, of course, of the vital fact that the counselee is a whole person whose problems cannot always be divided neatly into the categories organic and inorganic (or into categories of misreading or misleading). There are often elements of both. And most assuredly the organic affects the nonorganic and vice versa.

"For God hath not given us the spirit of fear; but of power, and of love, and of a sound mind" (2 Timothy 1:7). The word for *power* in this verse comes from the same Greek word we get the word *dynamite* from! The Holy Spirit should exert a powerful, life-changing effect upon our lives. Why doesn't the Holy Spirit do its job in the lives of some brethren? Because they don't let it operate. First Thessalonians 5:19 (KJV) says, "Quench not the Spirit." This means don't suppress, or stifle, the operation of God's Holy Spirit in your life. How could one do this? The Bible gives the answer in Ephesians 4. There is one body and one Spirit (verse 4). Neither God's church nor God's people are to have a split personality. The function of the ministry is to ground us in the Messiah's character so that we will not be carried about with doctrinal changes. Ephesians 4:11–14 (NIV) says,

> So, Christ himself gave the apostles, the prophets, the evangelists, the pastors and teachers, to equip his people for works of service, so that the body of Christ may be built up until we all reach unity in the faith and in the knowledge of the Son of God and become mature, attaining to the whole measure of the fullness of Christ. Then we will no longer be infants, tossed back and forth by the waves, and blown here and there by every wind of teaching and by the cunning and craftiness of people in their deceitful scheming.

In the past, we were all mentally deranged. With the receipt of the Holy Spirit, we have the power to put off the old mentally and spiritually sick man and put on the new man. That's the way the Holy Spirit's dynamic power should work. But why doesn't it operate in some cases? Because some of us succumb to corrupt communication, bitterness, wrath, anger, clamor, and evil speaking against our brethren. The result of this is the grieving of the Holy Spirit (Ephesians 4:25–31 KJV). Instead, verse 32 says, "And be ye kind one to another, tenderhearted, forgiving one another, even as God for Christ's sake hath forgiven you." The Holy Spirit is quenched when we attack our brethren and fail to love them.

A man recently baptized said to me, "It still amazes me at the warmth and charity that practically everyone who is privileged to know God's Truth shows."

John 13:35 in action is a beautiful thing to behold. As psychologists say, a warm, understanding relationship in the family is the best prevention for mental schizophrenia. The same holds true for spiritual schizophrenia. A warm, family relationship in the church of God is the best prescription for spiritual schizophrenia.

Shock treatment and drug therapy are not the answer to this problem. The love of the Savior is the only solution. "True holiness" (Ephesians 4:24) is speaking the truth in love to your brethren. There are going to be problems and quarrels between people, even in the church. However, we must bury our contentions, problems, and gripes by sundown (Ephesians 4:26). The surest road to spiritual schizophrenia is to let problems fester, to let your anger and peevishness continue past sundown. This gives a place to the devil and allows him to enter our mind as a "Mr. Hyde."

I want to take a look at the demon of schizophrenia, Imp# 1, delusion; Imp# 2, hallucination; Imp # 3, disorganize thinking (speech); Imp # 4, gross disorganized or abnormal motor behavior, and Imp# 5, negative symptoms.

Imp #1, delusion, is when you have fixed beliefs that are not amenable to change in the light of conflicting evidence. Delusions are bizarre thoughts that are generally accepted as reality or rational argument. Although bizarre delusions are considered to be especially characteristic of schizophrenia, "bizarreness" may be difficult to judge, especially across different cultures. Delusions are deemed bizarre if they are clearly implausible and not understandable and do not derive from ordinary life experiences. An example of a bizarre delusion is a person's belief that a stranger has removed his or her internal organs and has replaced them with someone else's organs without leaving any wounds or scars. Delusions that express a loss of control over mind or body are generally considered to be bizarre; these include a person's belief that his or her thoughts have been taken away by some outside force ("thought withdrawal"), that alien thoughts have been put into his or her mind ("thought insertion"), or that his or her body or actions are being acted on or manipulated by some outside force ("delusions of control").

An example of a nonbizarre delusion is a person's false belief that he or she is under surveillance by the police. I know a young man who studied Homeland Security and emergency management. After completing school, he found a job. He found it difficult to hold down a job, and conversations were coincidental. He would do something when he got home, and someone would make mention of something similar. He would then immediately think that a camera and microphones were in his room and the house. He even stopped listening to his radio, thinking that his conversations were being recorded.

HALLUCINATIONS

Hallucinations, Imp #2, may occur in any sensory modality (auditory, visual, olfactory, gustatory, and tactile), but auditory hallucinations are by far the most common in schizophrenia. Auditory hallucinations are usually experienced as voices, whether familiar or unfamiliar, that are perceived as distinct from the person's own thoughts. The hallucinations must occur in the context of a clear sensorium; those that occur while falling asleep (hypnagogic) or waking up (hypnopompic) are considered to be within the range of normal experience.

Isolated experiences of hearing one's name called or experiences that lack the quality of an external percept (e.g., a humming in one's head) should also not be considered as symptomatic of schizophrenia or any other psychotic disorder.

Hallucinations may be a normal part of religious experience in certain cultural contexts. Certain types of auditory hallucinations (such as two or more voices conversing with one another or voices maintaining a running commentary on the person's thoughts or behavior) have been considered to be particularly characteristic of schizophrenia.

Hallucinations, in the secular world, are often misunderstood—even by medical doctors. Let's start with a common secular definition, in layman's language, of *hallucinations*. "Hallucinations are false or distorted sensory experiences that appear to be real perceptions. These sensory impressions are generated by the mind rather than by any external stimuli and may be seen, heard, felt, and even smelled or tasted." Notice two things: 1) This is a very broad definition and 2) hallucinations are "generated by the mind rather than by any external stimuli." Let's think about this from a spiritual perspective: a demonic force / spirit dictates, and you can hear it audibly and see it visually, especially when it is telling you to do something that's not of God or positive.

I will focus on hallucinations that I believe are caused by demons. But first, let's briefly discuss hallucinations that likely have nothing to do with demons or are only indirectly related.

There are many causes of these hallucinations, including being drunk or high or coming down from such drugs as marijuana, lysergic acid diethylamide (LSD), cocaine (including crack), phencyclidine (PCP), amphetamines, heroin, ketamine, and alcohol; epilepsy that involves a part of the brain called the temporal lobe (odor hallucinations are most common); fever, especially in children and the elderly; narcolepsy; sensory problems, such as blindness or deafness; and severe illness, including liver failure, kidney failure, AIDS, and brain cancer.

There is a wealth of information available on the internet on this topic. But there are other types of "hallucinations" that really are caused by demons. And it's important to distinguish between the two. The key to determining which type of "hallucination" you are experiencing is to remember that demons have a function in this world and their activities fulfill that function: "The thief [devil, demons] does not come except to steal, and to kill, and to destroy" (John 10:10 NKJV). They have no other purpose than to destroy the individual and those who are around him or her and are affected by the action and reactions associated with this spirit.

Their activities will attempt to cause you distress, get you to violate scripture, or harm you in some other way. They may try to get you to harm or kill yourself. They may try to get you to harm or kill other people. Before continuing, I should mention that hallucinations caused by legitimate medical conditions are not caused by demons even if they are distressing. Diabetics, for example, may experience disturbing visual and auditory hallucinations that are directly related to abnormal blood sugar levels.

Most demonic hallucinations are auditory. I have a friend who works at a crisis center. Clients hearing voices were an everyday experience. The voices usually said derogatory things about the clients and would tell them to do things that they shouldn't do. Since it was a secular program, she couldn't tell the clients that the voices they were hearing were demonic. But she does tell them, "Don't trust the voices."

The clients would almost always respond, "Oh, I know that!" They had gotten used to hearing them.

The content of these hallucinations are rather predictable. Two client examples follow: The first client said that the voices "call me stupid," "pick on me," "harass me," and "tell me to drink more." The second client said he heard voices telling him to "kill yourself," "hurt yourself," and "you need to die."

Some demonic hallucinations are the result of a spiritual stronghold but not all. The ones that are the result of a spiritual foothold are usually angry and harder to get rid of. In this category, I remember a young man who was molested by his psychopathic father. The young man would hear voices telling him to "kill the child molester." To get rid of the voices, the young man would need to make progress in terms of forgiving his father.

Demonic hallucinations that are not the result of a spiritual stronghold are easy to get rid of, at least for Christians. All you have to do is pray or rebuke the devil in the name of Jesus.

Prayer and rebuking of the devil may also work with demonic hallucinations involving a spiritual stronghold. Prayer is especially effective if you pray with another Christian. If so, the result will be temporary. The hallucinations will continue to recur as long as the spiritual stronghold exists.

It can be potentially dangerous to rebuke a demon when you are not truly saved. Acts 19:13–17 (NIV) says,

> Some Jews who went around driving out evil spirits tried to invoke the name of the Lord Jesus over those who were demon-possessed. They would say, "In the name of the Jesus whom Paul preaches, I command you to come out." Seven sons of Sceva, a Jewish chief priest, were doing this. One day the evil spirit answered them, "Jesus I know, and Paul I know about, but who are you?" Then the man who had the evil spirit jumped on them and overpowered them all. He gave them such a beating that they ran out of the house naked and bleeding. When this became known to the Jews and Greeks living in Ephesus, they were all seized with fear, and the name of the Lord Jesus was held in high honor.

The most common reason why Christians cannot get rid of recurring hallucinations is because of the spiritual stronghold of anger. The use of psychotropic drugs usually makes it impossible to learn to use the Bible to effectively deal with this issue.

It should be noted that medications often do make the hallucinations go away while you are taking the drugs. And this is true whether the cause is medical or spiritual.

There exist similarities between the clinical symptoms of schizophrenia and demonic possession. Common symptoms in schizophrenia and demonic possession, such as hallucinations and delusions, may be a result of the fact that demons in the vicinity of the brain may form the symptoms of schizophrenia. The hallucination in schizophrenia may therefore be an illusion, a false interpretation of a real sensory image formed by demons. However, auditory hallucinations expressed as voices arguing with one another and talking to the patient in the third person may be a result of the presence of more than one demon in the body.

Hallucinations involving sexual content are relatively rare, but they do occur in both sexes. I remember a woman who told me, "I get raped every night." She was, of course, not actually being raped. But she felt bodily sensations as if she was. This was clearly demonic.

Demonic hallucinations can occur in conjunction with demonic delusions as part of a spiritual attack. For example, one client heard her therapist's voice (me) and believed that what she was hearing was my thoughts. Of course, what she "heard" was disturbing to her and untrue.

I found this to be very interesting. It is very important to teach people not to be afraid of disturbing voices, images, feelings, or ideas that come from the devil; not to dwell on these things; and to never allow themselves to believe a lie.

In evaluating someone with hallucinations, there are several salient considerations.

First, hallucinations caused by a medical conditions can quickly become emergencies. So, early medical evaluation and intervention are of the utmost importance. Of course, most doctors cannot distinguish between legitimate medical conditions and the spiritual.

Second, is the person detached from reality? If the person is insane, he or she should not be left alone. Family monitoring and supervision is essential

Imp # 3, disorganized thinking and speech, appears in an individual who switches from one topic to another. Disorganized speech typically arises from abnormal thought processes. A person engaging in disorganized speech might quickly jump from one unrelated topic to another, engage in incoherent "word salad," repeat things another person says back to them, or appear to be speaking with nonexistent entities. Speech can be so disorganized that it interferes with a person's ability to communicate with others. Disorganized speech is a symptom of schizophrenia and is particularly common with disorganized schizophrenia.

Disorganized schizophrenia is characterized by disorganization in speech and daily behaviors. People with disorganized schizophrenia often struggle to care for themselves and engage in daily living activities and routines.

There are also those who believe schizophrenia is spiritual in nature, as in demon possession. This idea comes from the Bible's accounts of people whose symptoms appear to mirror schizophrenia. While demon possession is possible in some cases, it is unlikely to be the cause for the majority. Schizophrenics do not have a reaction to the name of Jesus, nor do they possess supernatural knowledge. Also, when the biblical accounts are carefully compared to cases of schizophrenia, the symptoms do not truly look the same. "And devils also came out of many, crying out, and saying, Thou art Christ the Son of God. And he rebuking them suffered them not to speak: for they knew that he was Christ" (Luke 4:41 KJV).

As with all mental health issues, schizophrenia might have several causes that are unique to each person. Although symptoms may be the same, the causes can differ. That is why it is important not to pigeonhole people with the diagnosis into "spiritual" or "physical" categories. Furthermore, while some patients may be guilty of malingering (faking or exaggerating their symptoms), that does not mean the problem is not very real for others.

Believers should be filled with compassion for those suffering from schizophrenia. We can think of it as a prison of the mind. People with schizophrenia and their families typically lack support from both the Christian and medical communities because neither has all the answers. Because the disorder has no definite scientific explanation, Christians often blame sin and withdraw from the schizophrenic and his or her loved ones. The church should minister to everyone, including persons with schizophrenia and their families. Those who struggle with mental illness should be considered part of a mission field. They need the gospel to help them understand where God fits into the picture and that there is hope in Jesus.

Although the Bible does not specifically address brain or psychological problems, it does refer to people being healed of all types of maladies. The Lord works not only through miracles but also through medications, surgeries, counseling, and environmental changes. He does not want anyone to remain in hopeless suffering, and He calls all to come to Him with their burdens to find life "Come to me, all you who are weary and burdened, and I will give you rest. Take my yoke upon you and learn from me, for I am gentle and humble in heart, and you will find rest for your souls. For my yoke is easy and my burden is light" (Matthew 11:28–30 NIV). The Lord also calls His children to extend love and the gospel to those who hurt, especially those who are the most vulnerable:

My brothers and sisters, believers in our glorious Lord Jesus Christ must not show favoritism. Suppose a man comes into your meeting wearing a gold ring and fine clothes, and a poor man in filthy old clothes also comes in. If you show special attention to the man wearing fine clothes and say, "Here's a good seat for you," but say to the poor man, "You stand there" or "Sit on the floor by my feet," have you not discriminated among yourselves and become judges with evil thoughts? (James 2:1–4 NIV)

The Bible says anyone who calls upon the name of the Lord shall be saved: "For everyone that calls upon the name of the Lord shall be saved" (Romans 10:13 NIV). Those who suffer with schizophrenia can have hope in Jesus for life more abundant.

I am the gate; whoever enters through me will be saved. They will come in and go out, and find pasture. The thief comes only to steal and kill and destroy; I have come that they may have life and have it to the full. I am the good shepherd. The good shepherd lays down his life for the sheep. (John10:9–11 NIV)

The Lord can use all things for their good.

Chapter 4

RIB 4: BIPOLAR AND RELATED DISORDERS

Bipolar and related disorders are separated from the depressive disorders in *DSM-5* and placed between the chapters on schizophrenia spectrum and other psychotic disorders and depressive disorders in recognition of their place as a bridge between the two diagnostic classes in terms of symptomatology, family history, and genetics. The diagnoses included in this chapter in the *DSM-4* are bipolar I disorder, bipolar II disorder, cyclothymic disorder, substance/medication-induced bipolar and related disorder, bipolar and related disorder due to another medical condition, other specified bipolar and related disorder, and unspecified bipolar and related disorder.

The *DSM-4* lists four major types of bipolar disorder: bipolar I disorder, bipolar II disorder (recurrent major depressive episodes with hypomanic episodes), cyclothymic disorder, and bipolar disorder not otherwise specified.

In order for bipolar I disorder to be diagnosed, there must be

1. one or more manic episodes in which the patient feels hyper, extremely "high," wired, or unusually irritable and gets into trouble, is unable to function at school or work, or ends up being hospitalized
2. during the manic episodes, at least 3 of the following symptoms present: feeling overly self-confident or even grandiose, needing significantly less sleep than usual,

being unable to stop talking, having racing thoughts, being easily distracted, being much more active socially or sexually, being much more productive at work or at school than usual, or feeling agitated much of the time; getting involved in pleasurable activities without thinking of the consequences (e.g., buying things that are not affordable or having unprotected sex).

Life events can trigger depression or depressive reactions. These include insult, rejection, or failure; loss especially of a loved one or object; life stress and change, especially if it occurs too often or too quickly; lack of positive, reinforcing, or rewarding events (or loss of the power of such events); success (when it is very taxing or stressful, or sometimes just before a success occurs); learned helplessness, in which a person discovers, as a result of numerous experiences, that he or she can do nothing to change life events; and irrational, unbiblical self-talk or misbeliefs.

Cognitive therapists have emphasized that triggering situations do not cause depression per se. Instead, depression is due to a person's mental attitude or self-talk (reactions, interpretations, expectations, and implicit beliefs) in response to such situations. Perfectionistic and rigid ways of thinking, often with logical errors (for example, blowing things out of proportion, taking things too personally, focusing only on the negative, jumping to conclusions) can distort views of oneself, the world, and the future. Depression follows and is likely to persist unless such distorted thinking is challenged and corrected, sometimes with the help of a counselor. Another is anger turned inward against the self.

Some mental health professionals, especially those with a more psychodynamic (Freudian) perspective, suggest that unresolved anger turned inward against oneself can result in depression. Such anger initially may have been directed toward a loved one or object that has been lost. Hurt may underlie the anger, and eventually this results in depression.

Depression is one of the most prevalent and serious mental disorders in the United States. It has been called the common cold of emotional disorders and appears to be on the rise, affecting up to 20 percent of the population at some time in their lives, with women being twice as likely as men to suffer from major depressive and dysthymic disorders (a milder form of chronic depression) but not bipolar disorders. More specifically, major depressive disorder as one type of clinical depression is the most frequently diagnosed adult psychiatric disorder in the United States, with lifetime prevalence rates of 20 to 25 percent for women and 9 to 12 percent for men or point prevalence rates of about 6 percent for women and 3 percent for men. In fact, the National Institute of Mental Health (NIMH) has noted that over nineteen million adult Americans will experience some form of depression each year, with depression being the leading cause of disability and annual associated costs totaling more than $30 billion! Depression also increases the risk of heart attacks and is a serious and frequent complicating factor in stroke, diabetes, and cancer.

Bipolar disorder (previously called manic-depressive disorder) with extreme mood swings or ups and downs and a vulnerability to future episodes has also received increasing attention in recent years. It is estimated that about 1.5 percent of the adult population has classic bipolar disorder, affecting men and women equally, but with the inclusion of subtypes, the prevalence can be as high as 5 percent or even 6.5 percent!

Both depression and bipolar disorder are therefore crucial ones to understand in order to be of effective help to the many who suffer from these conditions.

Bipolar depression refers to the "lows," or depressive phase, of bipolar disorder. There are many forms of depression. Unlike unipolar depression, bipolar depression is part of a larger condition known as bipolar disorder. Depression can have a variety of meanings because there are different types of depression. Clinical depression as a disorder is not the same as brief mood fluctuations or the feelings of sadness, disappointment, and frustration that everyone experiences from time to time and that last from minutes to a few days at most. Clinical depression is a more serious condition that lasts weeks to months and sometimes even years. Bipolar disorder, the larger condition that includes bipolar depression, is a lifelong, or chronic, illness. It's a condition that affects the brain in a way that can cause extreme mood swings that vary in length. People with bipolar disorder can go from mania (the "highs") feeling euphoric or revved up and irritable to depression (the "lows") feeling down or hopeless. These highs and lows are called "episodes."

It is well known that severe depression and bipolar disorder have a high risk for suicide. Some have described suicide as a current "epidemic," especially among children, prisoners, the elderly, young adults, and particularly teenagers. Risks are highest among men, especially those over sixty-five, people who feel hopelessness, and those who have experienced severe stress. Other factors associated with a high suicide risk include a prior history of suicide attempts, alcoholism, the presence of an organized and detailed plan for killing oneself, the lack of supportive family or friends, rejection by others, and, for many, the presence of a chronic, debilitating illness. Most counselors are aware that when counseling depressed individuals or those with bipolar disorder who may be at risk for suicide, it is crucial to ask openly whether they have been thinking of taking their lives and, if so, whether they have specific plans. Open discussion, sometimes followed by hospitalization or referral, can reduce the likelihood of suicide. Within recent years, depression has become so common, within the church and without, that many people are aware of its symptoms and potential for impacting lives and families. Bipolar disorder involving extreme mood swings is also beginning to receive more attention. Helping others to understand the basics of depression and bipolar disorder can be a first step toward effective treatment for people suffering from these disorders.

After many years of denial and misunderstanding, Christians are coming to recognize that depression and bipolar disorder are complex conditions. They can be effectively treated, but they are not likely to be dismissed by simplistic explanations or approaches to treatment.

Here are some important facts about bipolar disorder:

- It may affect as many as sixty million people worldwide.
- More than half of all patients begin seeing symptoms between the ages of fifteen and twenty-five, but it can begin at any age.
- There is no cure, but for many people, the symptoms can be controlled with treatment.
- Bipolar disorder is sometimes referred to as manic depression.
- Some people may experience mood swings that are less extreme than a full manic episode, known as hypomania.
- People with bipolar disorder often also have other mental health disorders.

For more information, visit http://www.latuda.com.

DOPAMINE

Dopamine is a chemical messenger in the brain called a neurotransmitter. It helps control movement in the body and is also linked to thinking and emotions. Dopamine has many functions in the brain, including playing an important role in cognitive behavior, voluntary movement and reward, and inhibition of prolactin product pertaining to sleep, mood, attention, and learning. A common hypothesis, though not uncontroversial, is that dopamine has a function of transmitting reward prediction error. According to this hypothesis, the phasic responses of dopamine neurons are observed when an unexpected reward is presented. These responses transfer to the onset of a conditioned stimulus after repeated pairings with the reward. Further, dopamine neurons are depressed when the expected reward is omitted. Thus, dopamine neurons seem to encode the prediction error of rewarding outcomes. In nature, we learn to repeat behaviors that lead to maximized rewards. Dopamine is therefore believed to provide a teaching signal to parts of the brain responsible for acquiring new behavior. Temporal difference learning provides a computational model describing how the prediction error of dopamine neurons is used as a teaching signal.

SEROTONIN

Serotonin is a chemical produced by nerve cells in the brain. This chemical, or neurotransmitter, acts as a messenger in the brain. It helps control moods.

1. It gives us self-confidence, a feeling of safety and security.
2. It causes us to feel sleepy.
3. It increases our appetites.

The part of the brain where it does each of these three things is a different part of the brain from the part where the other two things occur. Thus, for example, increasing serotonin in the part of the brain where self-confidence is will increase your self-confidence but not your sleepiness. Unfortunately, we have no medications to increase the serotonin in only one part of the brain. This explains why medications to increase serotonin in the brain can also cause increased appetite and sleepiness. Medications which increase serotonin in the brain, such as selective serotonin reuptake inhibitors (SSRIs), including citalopram, escitalopram, fluoxetine, paroxetine, and sertraline, and serotonin and norepinephrine reuptake inhibitors (SNRIs), including venlafaxine and duloxetine, give us more self-confidence and a feeling of safety and security. By the way, serotonin also exists in our gastrointestinal tracts. In this location, it stimulates digestion. This is why such medications can cause gastrointestinal upset. But they can also help constipation.

NOREPINEPHRINE

Norepinephrine is a neurotransmitter that's released by adrenergic nerve terminals in the autonomic and possibly the central nervous system that has such effects as constricting blood vessels, raising blood pressure, and dilating bronchi.

As a stress hormone, norepinephrine affects parts of the brain where attention and responding actions are controlled. Along with epinephrine, norepinephrine also underlies the fight-or-flight response, directly increasing heart rate, triggering the release of glucose from energy stores, and increasing blood flow to skeletal muscle. However, when norepinephrine acts as a drug, it will increase blood pressure by its prominent increasing effects on the vascular tone from -adrenergic receptor activation. The resulting increase in vascular resistance triggers a compensatory reflex that overcomes its direct stimulatory effects on the heart, called the baroreceptor reflex, which results in a drop in heart rate called reflex bradycardia.

"Bipolar disorder" is a name that first appeared in 1957 for a severe mental illness. Before that, the same illness was called "manic depressive illness" or "manic depression," though that name only dates back to 1921. Neither term appears in the Bible, but the Bible teaches us a number of lessons we can apply to bipolar disorder.

The exact cause of bipolar disorder is unknown, although science has demonstrated a genetic component to the disorder. There is also no proof-positive test for bipolar disorder or manic depression. It is diagnosed based on the symptoms displayed by an individual, which has led to some controversy. In popular culture, "bipolar disorder" has been used as an excuse for destructive or sinful behavior, and the label has even been used as a source of pride among the entertainment elite. Being "bipolar" has become chic, but to those who truly suffer from the disease, this trendiness has done more harm than good.

A Christian who suffers from bipolar disorder or manic depression should treat it like any other physiological disease. While God certainly has the ability to work miracles and cure any malady, He often lets us continue our journey with a "thorn in the flesh" to remind us that He is sufficient. In 2 Corinthians 12:7–9 (NIV), we read,

> because of these surpassingly great revelations. Therefore, in order to keep me from becoming conceited, I was given a thorn in my flesh, a messenger of Satan, to torment me. Three times I pleaded with the Lord to take it away from me. But he said to me, "My grace is sufficient for you, for my power is made perfect in weakness." Therefore, I will boast all the more gladly about my weaknesses, so that Christ's power may rest on me.

If a believer had diabetes, he or she would seek medical advice from trained doctors, take prescribed medications, and seek godly counsel on how to deal with both the physical and emotional symptoms. The same holds true for a believer with bipolar disorder. There can be no doubt the apostle speaks of himself. Whether heavenly things were brought down to him, while his body was in a trance, as in the case of ancient prophets, or his soul was dislodged from the body for a time and taken up into heaven or whether he was taken up, body and soul together, he knew not. We are not capable, nor is it fit we should yet know the particulars of that glorious place and state. He did not attempt to publish to the world what he had heard there, but he set forth the doctrine of Christ. On that foundation, I base my thought that through the process of counseling, we are to keep the client focused on Jesus.

Someone with bipolar disorder or manic depression might give in to the misperceptions caused by the disease and commit sinful acts. A person with bipolar disorder must treat those sins like any other person should. He or she should recognize his or her actions as sinful, repent, and seek forgiveness. Believers with bipolar disorder should never blame their illness for their actions. John 15:22 makes it clear that we have no excuse for sin we commit. Blaming this illness on sin is just a cop-out and not taking responsibility for your actions. Although my thoughts may at times be chaotic, irrational, or delusional, if I sin, I am still separating myself from God, and that is never part of God's plan for me. Bipolar disorder is certainly an explanation for bad behavior, but is it an excuse.

If someone went up to a Bible-believing Christian and said that he or she had been told that he or she has a "split mind," then the Bible-believing Christian might remember that the Bible says, "a ***double-minded*** man is unstable in all his ways" (James 1:8 KJV).

Then the Christian might tell the person that "God has not given us the Spirit of fear, but of power, of love, and of a **s**ound mind [*read* "whole mind"]" (2 Timothy 1:7KJV).

Then the person would realize that his or her problem was spiritual, not mental. With his eyes wide open, the person might ask the Christian, "What, sir, shall I do?"

The Christian might say, "Believe on the Lord Jesus Christ, and you will be saved."

And then the person might get down on his or her knees then and there and accept the Lord Jesus as his or her Savior and would then be delivered from the *demonic activity* that is causing his or her problems.

The person, set free and wanting to let somebody know about it, might go and tell someone else he or she knows is suffering from the same thing, and then that person might accept Jesus and be set free. And then that person might go and tell somebody else, who tells somebody else, who tells somebody else, until there are no more people with bipolar disorder or schizophrenics. How would the psychologists and psychiatrists make a living? They might starve to death! And we wouldn't want that to happen, now would we?

So, they come up with a kinder, gentler name for it, and say, "Take this pill and call me in the morning and the morning after that … and the morning after that." And so we follow the politically correct spin doctors who make us feel better about ourselves instead of telling us that something is broken so that we can get it fixed. And we let them do it. For shame!

Did you know that doctors don't have a clue what causes bipolar disorder? Did you know that according to doctors, bipolar disorder (and schizophrenia) is not a disease but a syndrome? Why then don't they call it bipolar syndrome? Why, because you might look in the dictionary and find out that a syndrome means "a group of signs and symptoms that occur together and characterize a particular abnormality or condition" (*Webster's Collegiate Dictionary*, Eleventh Edition).

That means that a syndrome is not a problem but a sign that there is a problem. So, they call it a disorder, meaning that something is "not in order," or out of whack. You already know that! They're being politically correct again. They don't want you to know that something is broken, and they can't tell you why, because if you knew that something was broken and that they couldn't tell you why, then you might seek help elsewhere, perhaps even from Jesus. And if you sought help from Jesus, then you would find it. And when you found it, then you would get better. And when you got better, then you might tell somebody. And we surely wouldn't want that, now would we?

Schizophrenia. Bipolar. Six of one, half-dozen of the next. Both mean that something is broken that needs fixing. Both mean that a person does not have a whole mind. Jesus says He can make you whole. By the way, bipolar disorder is often a result of a generational curse and even affects many Christians and their families.

Generational curses are negative character traits that are spiritually passed from one generation to the next. We should also understand that some negative character traits may be learned sociologically through following the models of our parents and peers. However, other, more embedded traits may be spiritually inherited even when modeling does not exist. The Bible uses the word "iniquity" to describe these negative traits (Lamentations 5:7). Our forefathers have sinned and left us with a bent toward their sins. The Hebrew word translated *iniquity* literally means "perversion." Instead of being "straight," according to God's standards, we have a "perversion" or "bent." It is not uncommon that people who suffer from a bipolar disorder also have biological parents who have suffered from the same disorder.

Learned or modeled behavior can be replaced with new thoughts and new habits. However, generational curses must be broken. In brief, we should understand that Jesus became a curse for us suffering for our iniquities as well as for our sin (Galatians 3:13). Therefore, we can, through confession, repentance, and declaration of faith, declare that the curses are broken.

Have you ever seen a family where the father has a problem with uncontrollable anger, his son seems to have been handed it, and the grandpa had the same problem? Or have you noticed that not only do you suffer from something such as persistent irrational fears or depression, but your mother and her father also suffered from it as well? There are many people today who are living under bondage that the sins of their forefathers have brought them under.

Exodus 34:7 (KJV) says, "Keeping mercy for thousands, forgiving iniquity and transgression and sin, and that will by no means clear the guilty; visiting (punishing) the iniquity of the fathers upon the children, and upon the children's children, unto the third and to the fourth generation."

Lamentations 5:7 (KJV) says, "Our fathers have sinned, and are not; and we have borne (been punished for) their iniquities."

This is beyond learned behavior; many children learn to be messy if their parents are messy. This is a spiritual bondage that is passed down from one generation to another. Some symptoms of a generational curse are a continual negative pattern of something being handed down from generation to generation. Often people who are adopted end up with the same characteristics as their birth parents, not because they were around their birth parents to learn how they behaved, but because they inherited their spiritual bondage. Some common symptoms of generational curses are family illnesses that seem to just walk from one person down to the next (cancer is a common physical manifestation of a spiritual bondage), continual financial difficulties (they continually hit roadblocks in their finances), mental problems, persistent irrational fears, and depression. Anything that seems to be a persistent struggle or problem that was handed down from one generation to another may very well be a generational curse.

I believe the reason God would punish the future generations with the sins of their fathers is because of God's bitter hatred for sin. He would require somebody who practiced witchcraft to be put to death (Exodus 22:18). He knows that one of the most prized possessions you have is your children, and therefore, it makes sin a lot harder to commit when you realize that you are not the only one that is being punished for it, but also your own children are going to pay the price for your foolishness. That's what I believe is the reason behind generational curses. The whole human race fell thanks to Adam's sin, for that matter.

Even after Jeremiah 31:29–30 makes it clear that believers are redeemed from generational curses, the next chapter in Jeremiah (32:18 KJV) clearly says, "Thou shewest lovingkindness unto thousands, and recompensest the iniquity of the fathers into the bosom of their children after them: the Great, the Mighty God, the Lord of hosts, is his name." Apparently, generational curses are still in effect, but for whom is the big question.

Ezekiel 18:2–3 (KJV) tells us,

> What mean ye, that ye use this proverb concerning the land of Israel, saying,
> The fathers have eaten sour grapes, and the children's teeth are set on edge?
> As I live, saith the Lord GOD, ye shall not have occasion any more to use
> this proverb in Israel.

(Note the keywords "in Israel"; this is referring to those who are in covenant with God, which means believers, not the rest of the world.) Obviously, generational curses are alive and well in the lives of those who are outside the new covenant with God (nonbelievers).

Just as other demons don't automatically leave at the time of salvation; neither do the demons that you get from your ancestors automatically leave you either. Let's say that you accept Jesus at age fifteen. Because you were born a sinner and outside of God's covenant, you were still living under the curses handed down to you, and demons can enter you through those curses. Once you've accepted Jesus, those curses are broken automatically, but often the demons that entered in before you accepted Jesus still need to be cast out. In other words, the curse is already broken, and there's no need for you to break any generational curses. But the demons who entered into you through those curses before you accepted Jesus may still need to be cast out. That's why it seems so many believers are living under generational curses, when the Bible makes it clear that we have been freed from any curses handed down from our forefathers!

To break the curse is to follow James 4:7: submit to God and resist the devil, and he will flee from you. Submitting to God means you have entered into this full surrender with Him. You have to be willing to fully surrender every part of your being to Him—body, soul, and spirit—along with your entire life.

Chapter 5

RIB 5: DEPRESSIVE DISORDERS

According to the *DSM-5*, depressive disorders include mood dysregulation disorder and major depressive disorder (APA, 2013). Most symptoms of depressive disorders involve the body, mood, and thoughts. These disorders can interfere with people's daily lives. They will have trouble with normal functions. It can cause pain and problems for both the people with the disorder and those who care for them.

Depressive disorders cannot be mistaken as just feeling blue or feeling down for the day because of issues that are happening in one's life. People with these depressive disorders have found that it is difficult making it through the day. It is found that most major depression can have manifested itself by interfering with the ability to work, study, sleep, eat, and enjoy once pleasurable activities ("Depressive Disorders," 2015). Persons suffering from depressive disorders may find that the symptoms can last up to two or more years and can be treated with medication.

Major depressive disorder (MDD) is a common mental health problem that is treated by many mental health practitioners. Cognitive-behavioral therapies have proven to be effective in helping restructure the cognitions of the client, which in turn reduces depressive symptoms. Research has shown that individuals with MDD who value spirituality tend to view the world in a different way than those individuals who do not hold spirituality as an important value in their life. Spiritual individuals have religious schemas, and therefore, it would be important to incorporate spirituality into the treatment setting. This pilot study, Integration of Spirituality and Cognitive Behavioral Therapy for Depression (2010), utilizes a manualized treatment approach that focuses on spiritual growth and decreasing depression through a spiritually informed cognitive-behavioral approach.

TYPES OF DEPRESSIVE DISORDERS

1. Disruptive Mood Dysregulation Disorder—Severe temper outbursts that can be manifested verbally and can happen at any time. This disorder can be labeled as chronic to severe. Let it be known that this mood dysregulation disorder onset must be before the age of ten years, and these moods are likely to change as the child matures (APA, 2013).
2. Major Depressive Disorder—The person is depressed most of the day, feeling fatigue or loss of energy or a feeling of worthlessness, just to name a couple. People with major depressive disorder will find that they feel this way every single day of their lives with no hope that they will improve.
3. Persistent Depressive Disorder (Dysthymia)—People who suffer with this disorder find that they are depressed most of the day. It may last one to two years. It is also found in disruptive mood dysregulation disorder as well. The *DSM-4* defines this as a chorionic disorder.
4. Premenstrual Dysphoric Disorder—Again, this disorder causes mood swings, feelings of sadness suddenly, or tearful and increased feelings of sensitivity. This person can seem irritable or angry. This disorder is mostly found in females.

This is just a short list of depressive disorders with key similarities. The most radical is the outburst that is found in disruptive mood dysregulation disorder.

Postpartum depression is much more serious than the "baby blues" (relatively mild depressive and anxiety symptoms that typically clear within two weeks after delivery) that many women experience after giving birth. Women with postpartum depression experience full-blown major depression during pregnancy or after delivery (postpartum depression). The feelings of extreme sadness, anxiety, and exhaustion that accompany postpartum depression may make it difficult for these new mothers to complete daily care activities for themselves and for their babies.

Psychotic depression occurs when a person has severe depression plus some form of psychosis, such as having disturbing false fixed beliefs (delusions) or hearing or seeing upsetting things that others cannot hear or see (hallucinations). The psychotic symptoms typically have a depressive "theme," such as delusions of guilt, poverty, or illness.

Seasonal affective disorder is characterized by the onset of depression during the winter months, when there is less natural sunlight. This depression generally lifts during spring and summer. Winter depression, typically accompanied by social withdrawal, increased sleep, and weight gain, predictably returns every year in seasonal affective disorder.

Bipolar disorder is different from depression, but it is included in this list because someone with bipolar disorder experiences episodes of extremely low moods that meet the criteria for major depression (called "bipolar depression"). But a person with bipolar disorder also experiences extreme high—euphoric or irritable—moods called "mania" or a less severe form called "hypomania."

Marital problems are the number one reason that people seek counseling in the United States. Depression is a close second. Financial difficulties are the main reason that people give as the source of their depression. I can understand why this is so, with the amount of debt that many carry today, but often this is only the tip of the iceberg. As a matter of fact, our financial problems may be a good indicator that many other aspects of our lives are out of control, all of which may be leading us to depression.

We all have days when we feel gloomy, down, bored, or wiped out. We may call this feeling a mild form of depression, but *discouragement* is perhaps a better term. To expect to live in this world without occasional disenchantment and gloominess is totally unrealistic. Virtually every major character of scripture had down, unhappy, or sad moments, including Jesus Christ. Just a quick reading of Psalms, Jeremiah, or Ecclesiastes tells us that there is much about life, even the life of the godly, which is depressing to the point of tears, sorrow, and confusion. Yet, God never apologizes for this. Rather, He informs us that He uses these very things to mature us into the image of His Son. James 1:2–4 (NIV) says, "Consider it pure joy, my brothers and sisters, whenever you face trials of many kinds, because you know that the testing of your faith produces perseverance. Let perseverance finish its work so that you may be mature and complete, not lacking anything."

In this passage of scripture, James tells us to count it or consider it pure joy when facing trials of many kinds, for this testing of your faith causes perseverance. In James 4:7, we are instructed to submit ourselves to the Lord and resist the devil, and he will flee. When people are battling with depression, it is a test of their faith. If they just hold on and not allow this thing to continue, it produces that perseverance because you resist the devil and he has to flee. Romans 8:28–29 (NIV) says,

> And we know that in all things God works for the good of those who love
> him, who have been called according to his purpose. For those God foreknew

he also predestined to be conformed to the image of his Son, that he might
be the firstborn among many brothers and sisters.

God knows that you are going through your bout of depression, and because you persevered, you will have to realize that all things work together for good. God predestined this a long time ago. That is why James 1:4 is so important when dealing with the imp of this disorder. Romans 5:3–5 (NIV) says, "Not only so, but we also glory in our sufferings, because we know that suffering produces perseverance; perseverance, character; and character, hope. And hope does not put us to shame, because God's love has been poured out into our hearts through the Holy Spirit, who has been given to us." The perfect life consists of happiness and fulfillment, free of all the effects of sin. It awaits us in eternity. The emptiness, sorrows, and incompleteness of this life are direct results of the principle of sin in this world. Even so, God uses these trials as a means of keeping us from becoming too comfortable in our present condition. The result is that, like Abraham, we too "look forward to a city with foundations, whose architect and builder is God." Hebrews 11:10 (NIV) says, "For he was looking forward to the city with foundations, whose architect and builder is God." We have great peace in Christ and many wonderful and beautiful things in this life to enjoy.

NINE WAYS TO PERSEVERE WHEN DEPRESSION PERSISTS

I have come up with nine ways to press through depression. I have found that these have worked for my clients. Each client reported back that most if not all of these helped them through the process of their depression in holding on to their faith.

1. Revisit the Past

   When you're depressed, your perspective of the past is colored by melancholy, and you are unable to see things accurately. Melancholic depression is a form of major depressive disorder (MDD), which presents with melancholic features. Although melancholic depression used to be seen as a distinct disorder, the American Psychiatric Association (APA) no longer recognizes it as a separate mental illness. Instead, melancholia is now seen as a specifier for MDD, that is, a subtype of major depressive disorder. Melancholic depression is often considered to be a biologically based and particularly severe form of depression.

   For example, if you are in a low mood, try looking back on those years when you experienced death thoughts and think that you felt nothing but depression for more than a thousand days. It's helpful to peek at your mood journals from that period to see that you did have some good days and good times scattered throughout the painful stretches, which means you will have good hours and days in coming hard periods as well. Also look at photo albums that bring you joy. Although you still may be struggling, it's possible to contribute a nice memory to the album.

2. Remember that Pain Isn't Solid

Going through mood journals is also a good way to remind yourself that pain isn't solid. I suggest to all my clients to start a mood/daily journal. You may want to start the morning with excruciating anxiety, but by lunch, you might be able to enjoy a nice reprieve. At night, you may even be capable of laughing at a movie with the kids.

3. Maximize Periods of Wellness

Most people who have lived with treatment-resistant depression or another chronic illness have learned how to maximize their good moments. During painful stretches, you may consider these moments to be the rest periods you need between bouts. Try soaking them in as much as humanly possible, and let them carry you through the difficult hours ahead. The word of God tells us in 1 Peter 1:5 to cast all our cares Him the Lord for he (God) cares for us.

4. Act as If

Author and artist Vivian Greene has written, "Life isn't about waiting for the storm to pass … It's about learning to dance in the rain." That sums up living with a chronic illness.

There's a fine line between pushing yourself too hard and not challenging yourself enough, but most of the time, you will find that you feel better by acting like you're feeling okay.

5. Embrace Uncertainty

You want to know when your medications will work and if you will be able to sleep eight hours again. You are wrestling for control over the steering wheel, and the fact that you don't have it is killing you. The flip side, though, is that if you can inch toward an acceptance of uncertainty and unpredictability to let go a little.

6. Stop Your Inner Meanie and Remember Self-Compassion

Like so many others who battle depression, you may find yourself talking to yourself in ways you wouldn't even address your enemy. You may even call yourself lazy, stupid, unmotivated, and deserving of suffering. The self-denigrating tapes are so automatic that you often don't catch how harmful the dialogue is until you say the words out loud to a friend or doctor. You can relieve some of your suffering by addressing yourself with the same compassion that you would offer a friend or a daughter.

7. Attach Yourself to a Purpose

When your depression gets to be unbearable, you will need to find a picture of your family and close loved ones. Tell yourself that you have to stick around for them. It's fine if you never wear one of those "Life Is Good" T-shirts. You have a higher purpose that you must complete, like a soldier in a battle. You must see your mission through to the end. Dedicating your life to a cause can keep you alive and give you the much-needed fuel to keep going.

8. Stay in the Present

If you can manage to stay in the present moment and focus only on the thing that is right in front of you, you can eliminate much of your angst, because it's almost always rooted in the past and in the future. When you are in a painful stretch, one day at a time is too long. You will have to break it down into fifteen-minute periods. Tell yourself that for the next fifteen minutes, your only job is to do the thing in front of you whether that's helping your child with homework, doing the dishes, or writing a column. When fifteen minutes are up, commit to another fifteen minutes.

It is important to recognize that depression is not the problem in and of itself; it is a response or reaction to something else. For that reason, scripture says almost nothing about depression per se. However, it has much to say about the root causes of depression.

The Bible teaches that depression is not caused by the circumstances of our lives, but rather by our unbiblical reactions to those circumstances (with the exception of certain physical problems and brain disorders, which we will deal with in a moment). This can be proven both biblically and by observation. Examples, such as the difference between the way Judas and Peter handled their sins, abound in scripture. In everyday life, we see people become bitter and constantly depressed over a crippling accident.

9. Inner Healing Prayer for Past Hurts and Painful Memories

Begin with prayer for the Lord's guidance and blessing as well as protection.

1. Use a relaxation strategy (e.g., slow, deep breathing; calming self-talk; pleasant imagery; prayer; and biblical imagery or verses) to help the client relax deeply.
2. Once he or she is deeply relaxed, guide the client to go back in imagination to reenact a past event that is particularly painful or hurtful still. Ask the client at appropriate times, "What's happening right now? What are you feeling or experiencing?"
3. After sufficient time has gone by, pray aloud for the Holy Spirit to come and minister His healing grace to the client in whatever way is needed or appropriate.
4. After some waiting, ask the client again, "What's happening? What are you experiencing or feeling now?"
5. Close with a brief prayer by both the counselor or client if possible.
6. Debrief the inner healing prayer experience with the client, and assign homework, like the inner healing prayer to the client if appropriate.

Unfortunately, the depressed person has usually not made one unbiblical response to his or her problems; instead, he or she has usually made a whole series of them, thus complicating the recovery process. Inappropriate thinking results in irresponsible behavior, which increases depression, which in turn stimulates more inappropriate thinking, and so on. "His own iniquities will capture the wicked, and he will be held with the cords of his sin" (Proverbs 5:22 NAS).

In other words, depression often stems from a downward cycle in which we begin with a problem and react to it in a sinful way, causing a complication of the problem, which is met by an additional sinful response, and so on. As we will see later, this cycle must be stopped and an upward cycle of biblical responses must be started.

As I have stated earlier in this chapter, severe depression and bipolar disorder have a high risk for suicide. Some have described suicide as a current "epidemic," especially among children, prisoners, the elderly, young adults, and particularly teenagers. Risks are highest among men, especially those over sixty-five, people who feel hopelessness, and those who have experienced severe stress. Other factors associated with a high suicide risk include a prior history of suicide attempts, alcoholism, the presence of an organized and detailed plan for killing oneself, the lack of supportive family or friends, rejection by others, and, for many, the presence of a chronic, debilitating illness.

Many counselors from both spectra are aware that when counseling depressed individuals or those with bipolar disorder who may be at risk for suicide, it is crucial to ask openly whether they have been thinking of taking their lives, and if so, whether they have specific plans. Open discussion, sometimes followed by hospitalization or referral, can reduce the likelihood of suicide. Within recent years, depression has become so common, within the church and without, that many people are aware of its symptoms and potential for impacting lives and families. Bipolar disorder involving extreme mood swings is also beginning to receive more attention. Helping others to understand the basics of depression and bipolar disorder can be a first step toward effective treatment for people suffering from these disorders.

After many years of denial and misunderstanding, Christians are coming to recognize that depression and bipolar disorder are complex conditions. They can be effectively treated, but they are not likely to be dismissed by simplistic explanations or approaches to treatment.

"Come to Me, all you who are weary and burdened, and I will give you rest. Take My yoke upon you, and learn from Me, because I am gentle and humble in heart, and you will find rest for your souls. For My yoke is easy, and My burden is light" (Matthew 11:28–30 BSB).

Jesus gives us the key here to depression disorders. He opens the door and invites us in to have rest in Him. Then He simply offers us His yoke. Allow Him to guide you. It allows you to learn of Him and to find rest in Him. What does Jesus say to us today? The same three verses. He says, "Come. I accept you. You don't have to suffer and carry your burden and heavy load anymore. As I am, so can you become. Free. Above all hurts and pains. The enemy cannot touch you when you are with Me."

Depression is not simply a medical problem or a mental problem. Depression is often a being human problem. While medical and emotional problems can and often do contribute to depression, for others, this illness has very significant spiritual components.

Depressive disorders and bipolar disorders are known as mood disorders. These mood disorders alter the mood of a person. It has been found that these disturbances can be intense and persistent enough to be maladaptive and alter a person's personality. These disorders are serious enough to cause great levels of impairment and can cause severe interference in one's adaptation to and functioning in the world as we know it. The American Psychological Association states that at least 10 percent of the American population will experience major depression at some point in their lives.

Major depressive disorder (MDD) is considered a severe disorder that is sometimes accompanied by psychosis and catatonia (APA, 2013). Finally, depression is one of the most common psychological conditions and is a normal part of living in view of losses and disappointments that we all will encounter in our everyday lives (Lemma, 1996). We all will find ourselves falling into mood swings, but if this goes on for long periods of time, a person should seek treatment for the disorder.

Mood disorders are clinical conditions characterized by a disturbance of mood or persistent emotional states that affect how a person acts, thinks, and perceives his or her environment. People with mood disorders often suffer from overwhelming feelings of sadness (depression), while others suffer from alternating periods of mania and depression (bipolar disorder). Mood disorders result from a damaged body and mind—wounded people with damaged lives.

No two people experience mood disorders in exactly the same way. Some people experience a few symptoms; others experience many. The severity of the symptoms varies across individuals and over time. Potential symptoms of mood disorders include the following:

- persistent sad, anxious, or "empty" mood
- feelings of hopelessness or pessimism
- feelings of guilt, worthlessness, or helplessness
- loss of interest or pleasure in hobbies and activities previously enjoyed
- decreased energy, feeling fatigued, or being "slowed down"
- difficulty concentrating, remembering, or making decisions
- insomnia, early morning awakening, or oversleeping
- reduced appetite and weight loss or overeating and weight gain
- thoughts of death or suicide, suicide attempts
- restlessness or irritability
- persistent physical symptoms that do not respond to treatment, such as headaches, digestive disorders, or chronic pain

A mood disorder is not the same as a brief period of sadness or a passing blue mood. A depressed mood that occurs in reaction to loss (e.g., the death of a spouse) or trauma (e.g., rape) is often referred to as a reactive depression. While in some instances, a reactive depression may be severe and require treatment, it is normally of short duration and is often self-correcting. In the mood disorders outlined before, the depressed mood arises spontaneously and is chronic (long-lasting), the symptoms are severe, and the individual is unable to function normally.

Chapter 6

RIB # 6: THE DEMONIC FORCE OF SUICIDE

T his demon is taking control. This week alone, there have been two people in the news who have taken their lives because of the spirit of depression and personality disorders. Suicide is the act of intentionally causing one's own death. Suicide is often carried out as a result of despair, the cause of which is frequently attributed to a mental disorder, such as depression, bipolar disorder, schizophrenia, clinical depression, borderline personality disorder, alcoholism, drug abuse, and so on. It is more likely to occur during crisis periods associated with upheavals in personal relationships because of the preceding factors and other reasons like unemployment, poverty, bankruptcy, and so on.

Suicide. The word has a frightening air of finality. Laden with hopelessness, despair, and tragedy, it is a word that everyone wants to keep at arm's length. "Only people who are really mixed up consider suicide"—maybe that's what you've told yourself. But then one day that word enters into your thoughts in a different way. You find yourself in an unbearable situation. You feel trapped and powerless. Ultimately, your mind and your feelings say "end it all," and that seems to be the only answer.

Suicidal behavior disorder is a proposed *DSM-5* diagnosis that would be assigned to individuals who have made a suicide attempt within the past two years. A suicide attempt is defined as a self-destructive act deliberately carried out where there is a clear expectation of death. Considering suicidal behavior as a condition independent of depression or other mental disorders is a paradigm shift, as suicidal ideation, attempts, and successful attempts were defined as behaviors associated with mood disorders and other mental disorders. It is noted that about 10 percent of people who commit suicide do not have a mental illness, and "most people" who have depression or another mood disorder do not attempt suicide (Reardon, 2013). These finding can be very debatable and must be considered critically. To state that 10 percent of people who commit suicide do not have a mental illness assumes that the individual was properly diagnosed or that a potential mental illness was ever self-reported to a health-care provider or associate (e.g., family or friend). It is also a major assumption to state that most people with a mood disorder have not attempted suicide, as attempts may be denied or hidden. Differences in neuroanatomy have also been noted in postmortems of individuals who have committed suicide specifically in the prefrontal cortex, which is associated with inhibition, self-regulation, impulse control, and consideration of long-term consequences, as well as altered serotonergic function However, causality has not been established and is most likely much more complex than the observed neuroanatomical variations (Courtet, Gottesman, Jollant, and Gould, 2011; Reardon, 2013).

Men are three times more likely to die by suicide than women (NCI, 2013; 2006). A large body of evidence highlights differences in the suicidal behavior of women and men, with more men dying through suicide and more women engaging in self-harm (Payne, 2008; Schrijvers et al., 2012). Women are also more likely to use social supports available to them, and this may deter them from dying by suicide. They may also seek psychiatric or other medical intervention more than men (Oliver et al., 2005). However, there has been a marked increase in self-harm by young men and a corresponding reduction in women, which has led to the female: male ratio for self-harm becoming more equal over time (Hawton et al., 1997; Cantor, 2000; Kapur and Gask, 2006).

The *DSM-5* indicates that risk factors for suicidal behavior disorder are mental illnesses such as bipolar disorder, major depressive disorder, schizophrenia, schizoaffective disorder, anxiety disorders, panic disorder, and PTSD; substance use disorders (especially alcohol use disorder); borderline personality disorder; antisocial personality disorder; eating disorders; and adjustment disorders (American Psychiatric Association, 2013). Chronic pain and terminal or chronic illnesses, which cause impairment and loss of physical ability, may be comorbid with suicidal behavior disorder.

Satan knows that in order to take control of the human population to demoralize the male population. He gets into the minds of the men and has them take themselves out. Remember God has given *man* authority, and when Satan can get the man out of the picture and strike him with mental illness, the number one tool is fear. Men maintain dominant social roles over women and other gender identities, which are perceived as "feminine" in a given society. Hegemonic masculinity refers to the ways in which dominant discourses about what it means to be a man, and this is likely to influence men's behavior, including help-seeking behavior. The dominant discourse of masculinity, for example, that men are "strong" does not lend itself easily to seeking support. Vulnerability is associated with femininity and is therefore seen as something to be avoided. In a review of the literature on gender and suicide, male suicide rates were explained in terms of traditional gender roles. Male gender roles tend to emphasize greater levels of strength, independence, and risk-taking behavior (Payne et al., 2008). Reinforcement of this gender role often prevents males from seeking help for suicidal feelings and depression (Möller-Leimkühler, 2002).

There are several accounts of suicide in the Bible. I would like to take a brief look at some of them to see what God's word has to say about this subject.

KING SAUL

Because of defeat by the enemy and great fear after being wounded, Saul chose to end his life, rather than face abuse by his captors. When his armor-bearer refused to kill him at his request, he took his own life by falling on his sword. First Samuel 31:1–6 (NIV) says,

> Now the Philistines fought against Israel; the Israelites fled before them, and many fell dead on Mount Gilboa. The Philistines were in hot pursuit of Saul and his sons, and they killed his sons Jonathan, Abinadab and Malki-Shua. The fighting grew fierce around Saul, and when the archers overtook him, they wounded him critically. Saul said to his armor-bearer, "Draw your sword and run me through, or these uncircumcised fellows will come and run me through and abuse me." But his armor-bearer was terrified and would not do it; so Saul took his own sword and fell on it. When the armor-bearer saw that Saul was dead, he too fell on his sword and died with him. So Saul and his three sons and his armor-bearer and all his men died together that same day.

The spirit of suicide can affect and effect those who are around you and cause them to follow. Most individuals do this in a private setting not to impose their self-torture on others.

SAMSON

In his great drive for revenge, Samson was willing to die when he killed the Philistines in the crowded temple that day. Braced between two pillars, he used his final strength to push them down and take his own life along with his enemies' (Judges 16:25–30).

JUDAS

In great despair and guilt after betraying Christ, Judas carried a burden that led him to choose suicide. His story is probably the most well-known account in the Bible on the tragedy of suicide. He was Jesus's own disciple. He walked with him. He was close to him, but yet he still didn't "know" him. And instead of repenting and seeking forgiveness after betraying Christ, he allowed the great burden of sin to lead him to this terrible end (Matthew 27:3–4).

Suicide is the perfect storm of spiritual warfare, where all three of our enemies as Christians converge. The flesh wants the pain to stop. The secular world would have us believe that it is a perfectly acceptable solution to our problems. And the Devil relentlessly brings doubt, distortion, and lies. As the evil mastermind behind spiritual warfare, Satan uses his two primary weapons: his lies over truth and darkness over light. Like a colossal chess game, he maneuvers his pieces so as to force us into a corner of hopelessness, pain, and despair and then offers suicide as our only way out.

In a tragic number of cases, he wins because like Eve in the garden of Eden, we are ill prepared against his evil devices. It shouldn't be that way, given that God has given us everything that we need for life and godliness that we might fight and win these and any other battles.

A central text of Scripture that addresses spiritual warfare is 2 Corinthians 10:3–5 (KJV). The weapons that we fight with are not physical weapons but spiritual and are mighty through God to the pulling down of strongholds. Ephesians 6:16–17 tells us above all to take up the shield of faith. Romans 10:17 (KJV) says, "[F]aith cometh by hearing and hearing by the Word of God," that we may quench the fiery darts (darkness and lies) of the enemy; the helmet of salvation (which protects our minds and thoughts) of salvation; and the Sword of the Spirit which is the Word of God.

Scripture records two occasions when an individual went one on one with Satan. In Genesis 3, Eve relied on her common sense. In Matthew 4, our Lord Jesus relied on Scripture as His basis of truth. In spiritual warfare, proficient knowledge and use of God's Word can mean the difference between life and death.

When we or someone we love is in this battle with suicidal thoughts, our first thoughts often turn to medical science, and to the degree that we are physical beings, it is certainly prudent to have a doctor rule out any medical issues that may be causing or exacerbating our condition and prescribe medications that might alleviate the pain or despair that we are experiencing. But to the degree that we are spiritual beings created in the image of God, should we not also consider a spiritual approach to the issues as well?

The truth of God's Word, which is the Sword of the Spirit, and the Shield of Faith are two of our most powerful weapons. First Corinthians 10:13 (ESV) says, "No temptation has overtaken you that is not common to man. God is faithful who will not let you be tempted beyond your ability, but with the temptation He will also provide the way of escape, that you may be able to endure it."

Romans 8:31 (ESV) says, "What shall we say to these things? If God is for us, who can be against us?"

Hebrews 13:5b–6 (ESV) tells us, "He has said 'I will never leave you or forsake you.' So that we can confidently say 'the Lord is my helper, I will not fear; what can man do to me?'"

These powerful truths are not to be read lightly but to be internalized, meditated upon, read prayerfully, and believed by faith. Many of the Psalms provide a road map that we can follow from deepest despair into the very presence of God.

Spiritual warfare is real. The ammunition is live. The casualties are real. Our enemy is crueler, more ruthless, and deadlier than we often realize. But greater is He that is in us than he that is in the world! May we as Christians take the battle seriously and be faithful to take up the whole armor of God that we may not only stand as good soldiers of our Lord Jesus but also bear one another's burdens and defend one another with the very real weapons we have been given.

I would like to give what I share with my clients who are dealing with thoughts of taking their own lives. I have found that if they follow these simple steps, they will live to tell their own story. In any treatment plan you must start with step 1.

STEP 1—GOAL SETTING

As a Christian counselor, you should do the following:

1. Define the counselee's spiritual status and the circumstances that have destroyed his or her hope for living.

2. Use Scripture to show how we belong to God and that He alone is the vital answer to our souls' longings.

3. Identify and address both the difficult situations and, where applicable, the counselee's shame-filled identity.

4. Increase the counselee's hope and competence. Should suicide occur, encourage the survivors in their grief work.

Observation and Identification of the Problem

- Define the counselee's spiritual status and the circumstances that have destroyed his or her hope for living.
- What is the counselee's spiritual condition? Unsaved? Saved? Nominal Christian or seeking maturity?
- What is the immediate crisis that has precipitated suicidal thinking or attempts?
- What coping skills have been used by your counselee during bleak times in the past? Why are those skills in danger of being overwhelmed this time?
- How clearly is the counselee thinking? Does the counselee ruminate over the same despairing thoughts without making progress? If so, the counselee is in extreme pain and, for his or her own protection, may need to be evaluated by a doctor for antidepressant medication.
- If a suicide attempt was made, how lethal was the method chosen? Was it a gun or jumping from a high place? Or was it a mild overdose of an over-the-counter medication?
- What support does the counselee have immediately available? If little support is available and the signs point toward serious risk of suicide, consider having the counselee hospitalized (see "When and How to Hospitalize a Counselee" in Step 4).

Hope: The Crucial Ingredient

The turn toward suicide hinges on lack of hope. This lack can be chronic, part of one's internal history. Or the hopelessness can be acute, that is, due to an overwhelming external threat to one's well-being. Chronic lack of hope marks one who, deep inside, feels incompetent to handle life. Acute lack of hope, in contrast, means that life has gotten out of control, and even though the counselee might feel competent, his or her emotional and spiritual resources have been drained. Of course, chronic and acute lack of hope can occur simultaneously. Those who struggle with chronic hopelessness are much more vulnerable to acute hopelessness from traumatic outside events.

For the Counselor

The potential for suicide is directly related to losing hope in one's circumstances, especially when the individual has a chronic sense of low effectiveness in mastering life.

Angel Thought 1

Keep in mind that the suicidal person has decided that life is unbearable. He or she feels cornered by life and sees no way out. This counselee feels cynical about his or her own dreams because he or she no longer has any power to realize them. He or she feels impotent and hopeless; everywhere they look, there is pain.

Angel Thought 2

Keep in mind that suicide occurs when there appears to be no available path that will lead to a tolerable existence. When circumstances look hopeless and an individual has little sense of personal efficacy in handling life, the potential for suicide rises significantly!

Hope is "an attitude toward the future, an assurance that God's promises will be kept, a confidence that what is bad will pass and that what is good will be preserved." Webster 2015.

Shame is the belief that one is irreparably flawed as a human being and thus deserves to be held in low esteem.

STEP 2—BIBLICAL INSTRUCTION AND ENCOURAGEMENT

Scriptural Characters Grapple with Suicide

Use Scripture to show how we belong to God and that He alone is the vital answer to our souls' longings.

Several characters in Scripture either committed suicide or wished for death.

- King Saul falls on his sword because he is both defeated in battle and concerned that the "uncircumcised fellows will come and run me through and abuse me" (1 Samuel 31:4).
- Abimelech asks his personal assistant to kill him because a woman has mortally wounded him, and he is ashamed to die at a woman's hand (Judge 9:54).
- Judas, feeling remorse when Jesus is actually condemned, hangs himself (Matthew 27:5).

- Elijah wishes for death in 1 Kings 19:4—he is afraid (v. 3), overwhelmed (v. 4a), and alone (v. 10).
- Chapter 3 of Job is devoted to his insistent wish for death. Job wants to be at rest, quiet (v. 13) and free from the demands of life (vv.18–19). He suffers and feels bitterness (v. 20). His way is hedged in (v. 23); he is full of fear, dread, and turmoil (vv. 25–26).

The Bible acknowledges shame, hopelessness, and pain!

Job reflects three common reasons that death becomes preferable to life:

- He feels overwhelmed at the demands of his life: "I can't go another step."
- He is wracked by enormous, unrelenting pain: "I can't take it anymore."
- He feels closed in, having nowhere to turn: "I can't see a way out."

Another biblical character who wished for death was Jeremiah. He wanted to die because he was constantly in a sorrowful mode: "to see trouble and sorrow and to end my days in shame" (Jeremiah 20:18 NIV).

Shame often varies inversely with hope in Scripture. The shamed person feels no hope that he will recover from being mocked or despised. Consequently, Bible characters cry out to God to protect them from shame and increase their hope: "Sustain me according to your promise, and I will live; do not let my hopes be dashed" (Psalm 119:116 NIV).

"Hope deferred makes the heart sick, but a longing fulfilled is a tree of life" (Proverbs 13:12 NIV)

God Meets Our Deepest Longing

A longing fulfilled, a thirst quenched, a hunger satisfied—these are the signs that God responds to His children. Hope flies on these wings. The problem with longings is that we tend to confuse the trivial, the important, and the vital. Trivial longings are those for material wealth, critical acclaim, or community standing. Important longings are those for the love of a spouse, children, or friends. The only vital longing is that for intimacy with God.

God's priority is to draw us toward this vital relationship. He may even disallow the fulfillment of our trivial and important longings if that is necessary to draw us toward true closeness with Him. In Him alone will we find the vital answer to our souls' cravings: "and my God will meet all your needs according to his glorious riches in Christ Jesus" (Philippians

4:19 NIV). God reveals Himself as the One who loves to meet our needs and give us hope. "Every good and perfect gift is from above, coming down from the Father of the heavenly lights, who does not change like shifting shadows" (James 1: 17 NIV).

THE SCRIPTURES ARE CHOCK-FULL OF HOPE

The whole of our Christian life is built on hope. God generously supplies us with reasons why we should keep on hoping when all our circumstances scream out to doubt Him and to give up on life.

- "For in this hope we were saved. But hope that is seen is no hope at all. Who hopes for what he already has? But if we hope for what we do not yet have, we wait for it patiently" (Romans 8:24–25 NIV).
- "I pray also that the eyes of your heart may be enlightened in order that you may know the hope to which he has called you, the riches of his glorious inheritance in the saints" (Ephesians 1:18 NIV).
- "We have this hope as an anchor for the soul, firm and secure" (Hebrews 6:19 NIV).
- Praise be to the God and Father of our Lord Jesus Christ! In his great mercy he has given us new birth into a living hope through the resurrection of Jesus Christ from the dead … Therefore, prepare your minds for action; be self-controlled; set your hope fully on the grace to be given you when Jesus Christ is revealed" (1 Peter 1:3, 13 NIV).

Scripture is filled with declarations that hope lies in God alone. Psalm 25:4–5 (NIV) says,

- "Show me your ways, O Lord, teach me your paths; guide me in your truth and teach me, for you are God my Savior, and my hope is in you all day long."

And Isaiah 40:31 (NIV) expands on this by saying,

- "Those who hope in the Lord will renew their strength. They will soar on wings like eagles; they will run and not grow weary, they will walk and not be faint."

Often, hope is conveyed by the idea of waiting on God: "I waited patiently for the Lord;

he turned to me and heard my cry" (Psalm 40:1). A hopeful person is strongly protected against suicide. This principle is a powerful tool for the counselor.

A suicidal counselee is often one who has ingested, over the years, many messages that have made him or her feel inadequate or ashamed. He or she is, after all, saying to him- or herself, "You never do anything right. You don't deserve to live." Further, Satan strives intently to deepen one's feelings of inadequacy or shame with his incessant accusations.

One counselee who had debt troubles said, "All I'm good for is to ruin my family's finances." This person, who had many gifts, had fallen prey to the lie of "You're nothing but_____" (Each counselee will fill in the blank of a similar statement with the most damaging self-description possible.)

Practical Help for Today

Identify and address both the difficult situations and, where applicable, the counselee's shame-filled identity.

STEP 3—SHRINKING DISCOURAGEMENT AND SHAME WHILE BRINGING HOPE

1. Evaluate the counselee's current condition.
    1.1 Identify the abuses and deprivations affecting your counselee.
        Here, you determine the level of hope the counselee feels. Suicide most commonly occurs among those who have suffered physical, emotional, or sexual abuse or among those who experience deep deprivation of love from parents or family. What has been your counselee's background in these areas? What does your counselee feel his or her life is lacking? Is the lack real or exaggerated or imagined?
    1.2 Identify the degree to which your counselee has a chronically low sense of competence. Here, you are determining how deep your counselee's sense of inadequacy and shame is. To what degree is your counselee filled with self-blame? Does the counselee focus primarily on his or her failures, real or imagined? Does he or she feel unlovable? Does he or she feel others' lives would be better without his or her presence? To what degree does, he or she hold him- or herself responsible for situations not fully under his or her control?
2. Define solutions to the immediate situation.
    Once you evaluate these questions, lead the counselee in the following directions:

2.1 Christianity admits no impossible situations or ultimate deprivation. Because Christ is the way, there is always a way through hopelessness (see 2 Corinthians 12:9). Not only is there, in Christ, no ultimate impossible situation or deprivation, there is ultimate resolution and provision. A fallen world is not final. In a fallen world, deprivations and disappointments are numerous. But they do not gain finality by being numerous. Christ alone is final. A fallen world must give way to heaven, the place of ultimate provision.

2.2 Address shame by arguing with it—that is, offer perspectives that counter shame, especially those that emphasize your counselee's true identity in Christ. Explore with your counselee what the Scriptures say about who he or she became at salvation.

2.3 Further attack shame by exposing its hidden strategies: "What is my counselee getting out of believing shame's lies and accusations?" Example: A counselee may hang on to a shame-filled self-concept in order to avoid hope. Why? Because hope means being vulnerable. A hopeful person opens up to life, including both its joys and disappointments.

Helping Your Counselee Think Clearly

- Get a no-suicide agreement from your counselee.
- Put it in writing!
- Date it!
- Have them say, "I, (name), promise not to take my life, and if I feel I may not be able to keep this promise, I will call. This commitment is to remain effective indefinitely."
- Give your counselee a copy, and keep one for yourself.
- Reinforce this agreement at each session.

Most suicidal counselees are thinking in a circle: *I'm worthless, Life hurts, I feel more worthless, Life hurts still more, I feel utterly worthless,* and so on. All the strategies seek to break this circle. In addition, the following exercise may prove valuable: write words of biblically based encouragement on slips of paper. You might choose words like "beloved," "accepted," "precious," "enjoyed," and "delighted in." Come up with ten to fifteen words, and place them in a bag. Have the counselee pick a word randomly from the bag at the beginning of each session.

STEP 4—WHEN AND HOW TO HOSPITALIZE A COUNSELEE

(Refer to "Signs that a Suicide Attempt Might Be Possible or Imminent")
When?

- You should hospitalize your counselee when signs 1 and 2 are present, along with at least one other sign. Also note whether your counselee feels little or no increase in hope.
- You should hospitalize your counselee when sign 3 is present, and you sense little or no increase in your counselee's the level of hope.
- Explain to your counselee why you feel hospitalization is important. Use the preceding "why" factors as the basis for your explanation.
- Have a family member call ahead to a hospital with a mental health program. The family member should inform the hospital personnel that your counselee has agreed to voluntarily admit him- or herself. If a family member cannot be relied on to do this, you should do it yourself.
- If your counselee will not agree to a voluntary admission, a family member will need to see a county magistrate and declare that the counselee is a danger to him- or herself and needs to be involuntarily admitted to a hospital. The magistrate will have a county sheriff or deputy escort the counselee to the hospital. Of course, this procedure is quite invasive, and a voluntary admission should be sought if at all possible.

LIFETIME PRINCIPLES FOR GROWTH

Increase the counselee's hope and competence. Should suicide occur, encourage the survivors in their grief work.

PRINCIPLES FOR INCREASING THE COUNSELEE'S HOPE

Nothing is stronger than God's promises.

Both His unchanging purposes and His unshakable covenant with us make it impossible for Him to go back on His word. Thus, "we have this hope as an anchor for the soul, firm and secure" (Hebrews 6:19a). The soul is not self-anchoring. It needs something outside itself on which to fasten. Counselors should ask themselves, "To what is my counselee actually anchored?" Many depressive or suicidal counselees are anchoring to the reassurances of others that they are worthwhile. Always encourage the counselee to anchor him- or herself in Christ, the ultimate Shepherd.

The counselee needs to learn to live from the future. "God wages war on our despair by loving us into the future and by opening us up to infinite possibilities. The person, from the believer's point of view, is a pilgrim, a sign of what is to come. Thus, it is that we are invited to live not in the future, but from it." Living from the future means refusing to define ourselves as less than what we will be when we stand before God. Living from the future means living at the edge of glory and rejecting the attempts made by the Lord, the flesh, or the devil to cut us down.

PRINCIPLES FOR INCREASING THE COUNSELEE'S COMPETENCE

Help your counselee develop a deep belief in God's grace.

Grace simply means that God's favor always rests on His children. Under no conditions will that favor be replaced by condemnation (Romans 8:1). How does this increase competence? Grace conveys an invitation toward freedom. Grace engenders freedom to risk, to fail, to love, to grow, and even to soar (Isaiah 40:31). The result? Enlarged liberty to move; more space in which to experiment with new, godlier ways of living; a liberation of laughter; a deepening of relationships; the freedom to risk confronting and forgiving. However, legalism—a denial of grace—narrows movement. It constricts one's space. There is no room to try, to fail, let alone to soar. A person's feeling of competence plummets, and this makes one more vulnerable, under the right conditions, to suicide. In the psychological situation of suicide, the interaction of a low sense of competence and external threat results in a highly constricted space of free movement. This is equivalent, of course, to a low level of hope. To a person in this situation, there seems to be no course of action left.

With the counselee's help, construct assignments that gradually build a greater sense of both freedom and competence. For example, have your counselee make two lists, one entitled, "Things I've Always Wanted to Do" and the other, "Things I've Always Wanted to Say." With your prompting, the counselee can brainstorm as many items as he or she'd like. (When brainstorming, all ideas are worthwhile, for the time being.) Then edit each list. Which items bring the most hope to the counselee? Which ones are more likely to happen in the near future? Which ones have to be seen as distant (but still feasible) dreams? How can each be prayed for?

GRIEVING SUICIDE

The grief of those left behind after a suicide is complicated by larger amounts of anger and guilt than grief over other forms of death. Even so, working through grief from suicide usually involves the same basic elements of normal grief work: Grief work is emancipation from the bondage to the deceased, readjustment to the environment in which the deceased is missing, and the formation of new relationships.

Use these three elements—freedom from bondage to the deceased, readjustment to the world in which the deceased is absent, and the formation of new relationships—as a three-phase structure for counseling those grieving a loss due to suicide.

PHASE 1—FREEDOM FROM BONDAGE TO THE DECEASED

This means refusing to live as though the deceased were still around or would come back while still honoring the memory of that person.

Those in the aftermath of suicide may develop illusory thoughts about their loved one's death, for example, "If I had been a better parent, spouse, friend, son, or daughter, this wouldn't have happened." The fact is that people who kill themselves inevitably have options they haven't taken. Many are the forks in the road that lead away from suicide. Killing oneself involves many choices, conscious and unconscious, to avoid constructive options.

The more one can get rid of illusory thinking about another's suicide, the less one will be in bondage to the deceased.

PHASE 2—READJUSTMENT TO A LIFE WITHOUT THE DECEASED

1. Many people feel guilty about resuming life after a loved one's suicide. They feel that, no matter how long they wait, they are somehow trivializing the death if they go on with their lives. However, putting one's life on hold simply compounds one form of death with another.
2. Suicide may express considerable anger at those left behind. It is an act of rage whereby "the suicidal person places his psychological skeleton in the survivor's closet." Reardon, S. (2013). Readjusting to life after another's suicide means that the survivor must firmly refuse any responsibility for the "skeleton."

For example, a man who committed suicide after his wife confessed a sin against him was seeking to punish her endlessly. Her task was to take no responsibility for his action and to use God's path (repentance and confession), not her husband's (endless guilt and self-recrimination), to deal with her sin. She could feel great sorrow over his death without feeling that her hand had held the death instrument.

PHASE 3—BUILDING NEW RELATIONSHIPS

This may include deeper relationships with one's children, new friendships, or a new marriage. In any case, new relationships represent a statement that a loved one's destructive decision does not prevent the survivors' making the constructive ones.

Caution! While a counselor should provide reassurance to the suicidal counselee, that reassurance must never become a substitute for God's. After pointing the counselee toward God, the counselor must take care not to get his own needs met by the counselee's appreciation of him, should that come.

DEALING WITH REAL GUILT AFTER A SUICIDE

Real guilt, not the false kind, may stalk friends and family of the deceased after a suicide. Suicides do not occur in a vacuum. Frequently, the deceased comes from a dysfunctional family or social group that greatly compounded his or her pain. The counselor must help those who carry real guilt through the following steps:

- admit their contribution to the situation
- confess their sin(s) to God (1 John 1:9)
- stop denying whatever responsibility that is theirs for the tragedy

DOES THE PERSON WHO COMMITS SUICIDE LOSE HIS SALVATION?

Suicide is a sin, just like killing another person (Exodus 20:13). That includes killing oneself. But Christ died for *all* of our sins! If a person who has trusted Him for salvation commits suicide, he or she will in spite of that be saved. Two of the many passages that confirm this are John 6:37–40 and Romans 8:38–39:

Thus, our Lord will not drive anyone away who comes to Him! Notice that He takes it a step further and declares that He will not lose any that the Father has given Him and that He will raise them up in the last day!

HOMEWORK

Many counselees feel a low sense of competence because they are afraid to change the way they relate to a key person in their lives—usually a spouse, sometimes a parent. After determining who this person is, have your counselee write out an ideal dialogue with this person. Your counselee, in the safety of a writing assignment, can express anything and everything he or she has wanted to say.

When the counselee brings this to the next session, discuss with him or her what would be scary about saying these things to this key person. Help your counselee discover how and why he or she may have exaggerated this person's power. You can find this list and much more at http://www.intothyword.org; search for "suicide."

As a counselor, I have seen many Christians who wish they could shake off the chains of depression, anxiety, and other emotional constraints, even while they continue going to church and loving God. The Bible is full of normal people who felt despair at deep levels. After the flood, the Bible says Noah's family found him drunk and naked in his tent. One commentary said that maybe being in a flood was a really stressful experience after all. King David was very open about his depressed state, and Elijah bluntly asked God to kill him so he didn't have to keep living anymore. Depression isn't anything new to people who love God, so let's not act like it's just a modern-day curse.

Feeling depressed to the point of not wanting to live is not a reflection of one's devotion or depth of faith. Feeling suicidal is always about much more than just our faith. There are numerous compounding layers that lead people to want to harm themselves.

A counselor is trained to know the difference between common thoughts of hating life and thoughts that could lead to actions that might actually result in a suicide. Again, there is no need to struggle alone with intrusive thoughts. Most people do see improvement and go on to live lives of contentment and hope. Let us stop relating people's level of faith to their mental health status. People can love God and still be affected by the messiness of this world. My thoughts and prayers are with all of those who are under the weight of depression today, and my hope of freedom goes with them as well.

I practice cognitive-behavioral therapy (CBT), which is solution-focused psychotherapy, enabling clients to learn skills that they can continue to utilize to improve the quality of their life. From a Christian perspective, cognitive therapy can be integrated as an effective resource for those seeking answers in their life and as a means of changing and gaining control over faulty thinking and behaviors. A combination of the following strategies has been proven to be effective therapeutic treatments for stress and anxiety disorders: abdominal breathing training, muscle relaxation training, cognitive restructuring, systematic desensitization, and in vivo exposure.

CBT focuses on the development of personal coping strategies that target solving current problems and changing unhelpful patterns in cognitions (e.g., thoughts, beliefs, and attitudes), behaviors, and emotional regulation. It was originally designed to treat depression and is now used for a number of mental health conditions, for example, anxiety.

The CBT model is based on the combination of basic principles from behavioral and cognitive psychology. This wave of therapy has been termed the second wave. Behavioral therapy is thus now referred to as the first wave. The most recent wave is the third wave, containing the mindfulness-based therapies. CBT sits firmly within the second wave. It is different from historical approaches to psychotherapy, such as the psychoanalytic approach, where the therapist looks for the unconscious meaning behind the behaviors and then formulates a diagnosis. Instead, CBT is a "problem-focused" and "action-oriented" form of therapy, meaning it is used to treat specific problems related to a diagnosed mental disorder. The therapist's role is to assist the client in finding and practicing effective strategies to address the identified goals and decrease symptoms of the disorder. CBT is based on the belief that thought distortions and maladaptive behaviors play a role in the development and maintenance of psychological disorders and that symptoms and associated distress can be reduced by teaching new information-processing skills and coping mechanisms.

Cognitive therapy (CT), or cognitive behavior therapy (CBT) was pioneered by Dr. Aaron T. Beck in the 1960s, while he was a psychiatrist at the University of Pennsylvania. Having studied and practiced psychoanalysis, Dr. Beck designed and carried out several experiments to test psychoanalytic concepts of depression. Fully expecting the research would validate these fundamental concepts, he was surprised to find the opposite.

As a result of his findings, Dr. Beck began to look for other ways of conceptualizing depression. He found that depressed patients experienced streams of negative thoughts that seemed to arise spontaneously. He called these cognitions "automatic thoughts." He found that the patients' automatic thoughts fell into three categories. The patients had negative ideas about themselves, the world, and the future.

Dr. Beck began helping patients identify and evaluate these automatic thoughts. He found that by doing so, patients were able to think more realistically. As a result, they felt better emotionally and were able to behave more functionally. When patients changed their underlying beliefs about themselves, their world, and other people, therapy resulted in long-lasting change. Dr. Beck called this approach "cognitive therapy." It has also become known as "cognitive behavior therapy."

The cognitive therapy process identifies distorted thoughts and perceptions that contribute to the anxiety, which are then challenged and redirected. Here are some of the basic fundamentals:

1. Help the client identify the sources of stress and anxiety by asking the client to keep a journal of daily events, activities, thoughts, feelings, and physical discomfort and the severity. This helps to make connections between negative thoughts and the resulting emotions and behaviors.
2. Once a list of automatic distorted thoughts and fears are identified, begin to teach clients to monitor and challenge these with contrary evidence and reality. Using the Word of God is a helpful mainstay for this process.
3. Teach strategies to dispute the negative irrational thinking, substituting new ways of thinking, believing, and responding, and help them deal with reality.
4. The client then learns how to monitor their negative thinking, ruminating, and self-talk by having better control of their thoughts and thus over their lives.
5. Then they are able to identify, question, and change the irrational thinking and replace it with empowering, positive thoughts and beliefs.

Interacting with the cognitive beliefs that we hold are certain cognitive processes that keep data in or out of our awareness and also determine the meaning we make of the data available to us. The three most important cognitive processes are selective attention, attributions, and cognitive avoidance processes. One of the aspects of Freud's theory that most therapists have accepted as having some validity, whether or not they accept the validity of the rest of his constructs, is his theory of ego defense mechanisms. Ego defense mechanisms are mental processes that serve to keep overwhelming or anxiety-producing data out of conscious awareness, either temporarily, or if the data would be extremely overwhelming, out of conscious awareness for long periods of time.

In a cognitive-behavioral model, emotions are considered to primarily be the result of the cognitions a person holds and the cognitive processes he or she engages in. Emotions are important for a number of reasons. They are an integral part of the total human experience, and it is important that a therapist recognize and respect them in order for a client to feel understood.

The core principles of CBT are identifying negative or false beliefs and testing or restructuring them. Oftentimes, someone being treated with CBT will have homework in between sessions, where they practice replacing negative thoughts with more realistic thoughts based on prior experiences or record their negative thoughts in a journal. Cognitive behavioral therapy has a considerable amount of scientific data supporting its use and many mental health-care professionals have training in CBT, making it both effective and accessible.

To understand CBT, we must first recognize where it came from. CBT was birthed out of two previously separate forms of therapy: behavioral therapy and cognitive therapy. Behavioral therapy was developed, most famously, by B. F. Skinner and was propelled into wide use by the needs of soldiers returning from World War II. Cognitive therapy was developed by Albert Ellis and Aaron Beck. They identified irrational thoughts and beliefs as the greatest cause of psychological problems. Beginning in the late 1970s, those who practiced behavioral therapy (behaviorists), recognizing the overly simplistic nature of their theories, began incorporating cognitive approaches into their therapeutic repertoire. This gave rise to cognitive behavioral therapy in the early 1980s.

In observing CBT today, the legacies of Skinner, Ellis, and Beck are still readily apparent. CBT recognizes that, just as thoughts must be addressed in order to change behavior, changing behavior inevitably helps in the process of changing thoughts. Part of the inheritance from [behavioral therapy] is that CBT considers behavior (what we do) as crucial in maintaining—or in changing—psychological states. For the CBT therapist this dual legacy is reflected in equal emphasis given to behavioral and cognitive techniques.

Christian counseling is a blending of psychotherapy or counseling efforts with the Christian value system, beliefs, and philosophy. It is a general term and does not specify the particular training of the counselor, nor the particular approach to the counseling. That is, licensed professionals as well as laypeople may identify themselves as Christian counselors, and they may differ widely in their styles and methods of counseling. The unifying factor is the reliance on Christianity (Christ-centered and Bible-based) for guidance and healing.

Cognitive behavioral therapy is a form of therapy that has been demonstrated by many research studies to be the most effective approach for a variety of psychological problems. The therapy relationship is collaborative and goal-oriented, and the focus on thoughts, beliefs, assumptions, and behaviors is key. In CBT, the goal is for a person to develop more realistic and rational perspectives and make healthier behavioral choices, as well as to feel relief from negative emotional states. Specific techniques, strategies, and methods are used to help people to improve their mood, relationships, and work performance.

Intervention studies have found that psychotherapeutic interventions that explicitly integrate clients' spiritual and religious beliefs in therapy are as effective, if not more so, in reducing depression than those that do not for religious clients. However, few empirical studies have examined the effectiveness of religiously (versus spiritually) integrated psychotherapy, and no manualized mental health intervention had been developed for the medically ill with religious beliefs. To address this gap, we developed and implemented a novel religiously integrated adaptation of cognitive-behavioral therapy (CBT) for the treatment of depression in individuals with chronic medical illness. This chapter describes the development and implementation of the intervention.

First, we provide a brief overview of CBT. Next, we describe how religious beliefs and behaviors can be integrated into a CBT framework. Finally, we describe religiously integrated cognitive behavioral therapy (RCBT), a manualized therapeutic approach designed to assist depressed individuals to develop depression-reducing thoughts and behaviors informed by their own religious beliefs, practices, and resources. This treatment approach has been developed for five major world religions (Christianity, Judaism, Islam, Buddhism, and Hinduism), increasing its potential to aid the depressed medically ill from a variety of religious backgrounds.

Christ begins to transform our mind from the very beginning of our new life, and it will be a daily process for us the rest of our lives. We become entrenched in our fears and riddled with a host of supporting thoughts that lead to a pattern of self-destructive mental habits. For years, we have heard and endorsed lies about ourselves, our experiences, and our view of our future. This process of transformation is a grace in our lives!

Contrary to a typical cognitive behavioral approach to therapy, it is not the goal of the Christian therapist to merely return a client to a "normal" or natural state of thinking about him- or herself, his or her experiences, and his or her future. In fact, a Christian therapist recognizes that, far from the end goal, the natural state of our mind is the problem! Rather, it is the Christian therapist's goal to partner with the Lord in what is already an ongoing process of that renewal.

Upon becoming a Christian, we gain a new view of self. The Bible has much to say about who we are. In Christ, we learn that God has chosen us; He has given us His own Son; He has given us a permanent place with Him. The lies we have grown accustomed to hearing have no place in our lives!

God's opinion of us makes all the difference and has the potential to change all of the dynamics that plague our natural mind with insecurities, rejection, and fear. Our view of experiences changes from this perspective, and we are continually reminded that God is working everything for the good of those who are called according to His purpose. Our view of the future is built upon both the renewal of our view of self and experiences, coupled with Scripture that reveals the hope of an eternal home with Him and with His people.

Let me wrap this up with this final statement and these Scriptures on CBT/C-CBT and RCBT

Romans 12:2 (ESV) says, "Do not be conformed to this world, but be transformed by the renewal of your mind, that by testing you may discern what is the will of God, what is good and acceptable and perfect."

And in 2 Corinthians 10:5 (ESV), we read, "We destroy arguments and every lofty opinion raised against the knowledge of God and take every thought captive to obey Christ."

These are biblical texts supportive of the cognitive-behavioral approach. God instructs us to guard our thoughts. Satan is the "father of lies" John 8:44 (ESV) says, "You are of your father the devil, and your will is to do your father's desires. He was a murderer from the beginning, and does not stand in the truth, because there is no truth in him. When he lies, he speaks out of his own character, for he is a liar and the father of …" If our minds are not firmly grounded in truth, then we are more susceptible to his deceptions. James 2:14 (ESV) says, "What good is it, my brothers, if someone says he has faith but does not have works? Can that faith save him?" This speaks of how our beliefs affect our behaviors.

At the same time, cognitive-behavioral therapy's goal of self-acceptance is not inherently unbiblical. We are accepted by God in our imperfection (Ephesians 2:1–10; Colossians 2:13; Romans 5:6–8). However, we are not left imperfect. It is important to balance the truth of our justification with the process of sanctification.

Cognitive-behavior therapy may have some helpful techniques for Christians seeking to take their thoughts captive or improve in other areas requiring self-control. It can also be useful in revealing the enemy's lies so that Christians are not duped into self-loathing or self-defeating behaviors. However, to be free of false thoughts and to truly grow, we need to be grounded in God's truth and sanctified by the power of the Holy Spirit.

Schema therapy is similar to cognitive therapy in that the focus is on correcting problems in a person's habitual patterns of thinking and feeling and corresponding difficulties in his or her behavioral coping style. The focus is on identifying and understanding and then challenging and overcoming the long-standing maladaptive patterns in thinking, feeling, and behaving that create obstacles for a person in getting needs met and attaining life goals. As with standard CBT, the goal is for the person to feel better and enjoy greater life satisfaction.

Schema therapy (or more properly, schema-focused cognitive therapy) is an integrative approach to treatment that combines the best aspects of cognitive-behavioral, experiential, interpersonal, and psychoanalytic therapies into one unified model. Schema-focused therapy has shown remarkable results in helping people to change negative ("maladaptive") patterns that they have lived with for a long time, even when other methods and efforts they have tried before have been largely unsuccessful.

The schema-focused model was developed by Dr. Jeff Young, who originally worked closely with Dr. Aaron Beck, the founder of cognitive therapy. While treating clients at the Center for Cognitive Therapy at the University of Pennsylvania, Dr. Young and his colleagues identified a segment of people who had difficulty benefiting from the standard approach. He discovered that these people typically had long-standing patterns or themes in thinking, feeling, and behaving/coping that required a different means of intervention. Dr. Young's attention turned to ways of helping patients to address and modify these deeper patterns or themes, also known as "schemas" or "life traps."

The schemas that are targeted in treatment are enduring and self-defeating patterns that typically begin early in life. These patterns consist of negative/dysfunctional thoughts and feelings, have been repeated and elaborated upon, and pose obstacles for accomplishing one's goals and getting one's needs met. Some examples of schema beliefs are: "I'm unlovable," "I'm a failure," "People don't care about me," "I'm not important," "Something bad is going to happen," "People will leave me," "I will never get my needs met," "I will never be good enough," and so on.

Although schemas are usually developed early in life (during childhood or adolescence), they can also form later, in adulthood. These schemas are perpetuated behaviorally through the coping styles of schema maintenance, schema avoidance, and schema compensation. The schema-focused model of treatment is designed to help the person to break these negative patterns of thinking, feeling, and behaving, which are often very tenacious, and to develop healthier alternatives to replace them.

When emotional needs, one's basic needs for affection, guidance, love, shelter, and safety, go unmet in childhood, individuals may enter adulthood with deficits in their abilities to find ways for these needs to be met, independently and through healthy relationships with others. Schema therapy is based on the belief that early maladaptive schemas form based on these adverse childhood experiences. These maladaptive schemas, which can be described as ways individuals interpret life events and the behavior of others, can later disrupt life. Individuals may make unhealthy choices, form toxic relationships, lack fully developed social skills, engage in destructive behavior patterns, have a poor sense of judgment, and experience feelings of worthlessness or self-doubt.

When I use schemas during my session with the counselee, I employ imagery through music therapy and meditation. I often use the open chair. This aspect of therapy attempts to help counselees identify variations in emotions and personality. In chair work, the person in therapy moves between two chairs, expressing different emotions and aspects of personality in each chair. Chair work can also be used to help a person in treatment imagine dialogues with family, friends, or significant others. In this type of chair work, a person might make statements regarding emotional needs while sitting in one chair and then move to another chair to play the role of a person who might meet these emotional needs. Imagery work is often conducted in conjunction with chair work. This moves me into another theory.

Gestalt therapy theory was developed and formulated by Fritz Perls (1893–1970). He based his idea on a whole being as connected to his or her environment. This theory works toward creating awareness of the here and now. The open chair is one of many interactive techniques used to help engage the client's feelings, thoughts, and behaviors. However, the Gestalt therapy was coined by Max Wertheimer in 1924.

The open chair or the empty chair has had quite a tongue-lashing over the years. Clients have given a piece of their mind to innumerable spouses, bosses, best friends, and dead relatives, thanks to this simple tool. But the chair is none the worse for wear, and millions of people have a greater understanding of their feelings and communication as a result of this method of counseling.

Another theory I would like to discuss is that of client-centered therapy. I'm also a fan of this therapy because of the humanistic side. It was coined by Carl Rogers in the 1940s and '50s. Rogers believed that people were fundamentally good. Rogers initially started out calling his technique nondirective therapy. While his goal was to be as nondirective as possible, he eventually realized that therapists guide clients even in subtle ways. He also found that clients often do look to their therapists for some type of guidance or direction. Eventually, the technique came to be known as client-centered therapy or person-centered therapy. Today, Rogers's approach to therapy is often referred to by either of these two names, but it is also frequently known simply as Rogerian therapy. It is also important to note that Rogers was deliberate in his use of the term *client* rather than *patient*. He believed that the term *patient* implied that the individual was sick and seeking a cure from a therapist. By using the term *client* instead, Rogers emphasized the importance of the individual in seeking assistance, controlling his or her destiny, and overcoming his or her difficulties. This self-direction plays a vital part in client-centered therapy.

COGNITIVE THERAPY'S COMPATIBILITY WITH CHRISTIANITY

Cognitive therapy brings many contributions to counseling. Brief therapy discourages a client from becoming dependent upon the therapist. In some forms of long-term therapy, such as psychoanalysis, often, a client never really changes but feels better because he or she has someone to talk to. Cognitive therapy aids in a person's independence and control in making effective choices in his life. This is a worthy set of principles for a Christian to adopt in seeking to be a biblical good steward of the time allotted to us.

This theme of independence is further helpful because rather than rely indefinitely upon the expertise of one person, clients learn to evaluate their own thoughts. They are taught to view their beliefs as hypotheses and to test the validity of their hypotheses by seeing if the data fits what they believe. This kind of approach trains people to follow the biblical principle of testing everything by the Scriptures. In 1 John 4:1 (NKJV), we read, "Beloved, do not believe every spirit, but test the spirits, whether they are of God; because many false prophets have gone out into the world." They are taught not to take at face value the words of any man who claims to be a prophet or preacher but to look to the Bible for what is true as the final standard.

Cognitive therapy is especially beneficial in counseling a client with depression: "It focuses on developing a detailed case conceptualization as a way to understand how clients view their world" (Corey, 2001, 328). It brings the client's personal experience "back into the realm of legitimate scientific inquiry" (Corey, 2001, 328). It is obvious that the client's background and personal insight into his or her situation and feelings about it are taken into account. In 1 Corinthians 9:19–22, Paul talked about the importance of understanding the background of a person, his or her heritage, and how he or she thinks. Paul then used this information to reach that person for Christ in the most effective way. In this respect, cognitive therapy agrees with the biblical approach.

In addition, cognitive therapy is useful in challenging a client's beliefs in order to change his or her behavior (Corey, 2001). This directly agrees with many passages of Scripture that address changing one's thinking about things in order to change mood and behavior. "Be anxious for nothing, but in everything by prayer and supplication, with thanksgiving, let your requests be made known to God; and the peace of God, which surpasses all understanding, will guard your hearts and minds through Christ Jesus" (Philippians 4:6–7 NKJV).

Here, Paul says that if a person is anxious, he or she should respond instead by praying and changing his or her thought process to one of thanksgiving about the things that he or she is petitioning the Lord about. The Bible says that the reward is a mind and heart at peace. Similarly, the Bible tells us to take every thought captive (2 Corinthians 10:5) and to renew our minds (Romans 12:1–2). As in cognitive therapy, we are to be active in changing the old thought patterns to ones that are true and fitting.

INCONSISTENCIES BETWEEN CHRISTIANITY AND COGNITIVE THERAPY

A major problem with the secular use of cognitive therapy is its use of constructivism, the belief that there are no absolutes, that people construct their own reality. This leaves only a pragmatic view of right and wrong. "Therapists can encourage their clients to reconsider absolutist judgments by moving toward seeing both 'good' and 'bad' elements in situations" (Corey, 2001, 322).

The subjective beliefs of the client are elevated as more important than objective faulty beliefs. Right and wrong are not counted as important as what works for the client. Constructivism says that if a belief is helpful for the individual, if it improves his or her affect, and does not harm others, it is functional. If used apart from a Christian perspective, cognitive therapy can be a surface approach, dealing only with eliminating symptoms that lead to depression and never with the root cause of difficulty. The Christian approach would involve getting directly to the underlying false beliefs.

Some cognitive therapy has been criticized as being too cognitive and downplaying, even undermining, emotions in the process. It does not encourage "emotional ventilation or emotionally re-experiencing painful experiences" (Corey, 2001, 331). In comparison, the Bible tells us in Ecclesiastes 3:4 that there is a time for weeping. It tells us to weep with those who weep (Romans 12:15), which implies that we are not only to experience the emotions that are a natural part of going through difficult things but to encourage others to do so as well.

Chapter 7

COGNITIVE BEHAVIOR THERAPY AND THE SPIRITUAL BATTLE

R omans 6:16 (NKJV) says, "Do you not know that to whom you present yourselves slaves to obey, you are that one's slaves whom you obey, whether of sin to death, or of obedience to righteousness?"

The apostle Paul defines strongholds as speculations or lofty things raised up against the knowledge of God. It is any type of thinking that exalts itself above the knowledge of God, thereby giving the devil a secure place of influence in an individual's thought-life. Second Corinthians 10:4–5 (NKJV) states, "For the weapons of our warfare are not carnal, but mighty through God to the pulling down of strongholds; Casting down imaginations and every high thought that exalts itself against the knowledge of God and bringing into captivity every thought into the obedience of Christ."

There is tremendous power in the way we perceive things and the way we think. A stronghold is basically like a pattern that has been burned into our minds that causes us to think or perceive things in a certain way. I have seen conditions taken to deliverance ministers that are clearly demonic, but the minister can only go so far and seems to hit a roadblock. Why is that? In many situations, it is a stronghold that needs to come down. Demons and strongholds are quite good friends and allies to each other.

Demons often promote us to build strongholds in our minds, and they use strongholds to torment countless people around the globe today. From my experience of ministering to the oppressed, I have found that there are two common strongholds that hold countless believers in bondage. The first one is an incorrect perception of who God is, and the other is an incorrect perception of who they are. I feel it is important to recognize and understand both of these strongholds in not only our lives but the lives of those to whom we are ministering.

Some of the common symptoms of this stronghold include the following:

- Lacking the desire for an intimate and close relationship with God and feeling that God is distant and cold, rather than intimate, loving, and personal. Irrational fears of God will hinder a person from drawing near to Him. They have an irrational and unhealthy fear of Him, which prevents them from drawing close to Him.
- A lack of love in a person's heart for God. The reason the world doesn't care about God is because they don't really know (perceive) Him correctly. If you find it hard or boring to spend time with God and would rather do other things, then you have an incorrect perception of Him that needs to be changed.
- Feeling unwanted and unloved by God. Many admit to feeling like God is mad at them for one reason or another. If a person wonders if God still loves him or her, it's a good clue that the person needs to change his or her perception of God.
- Even OCD can be driven by irrational fears of God. It can drive people into what they call perfectionism, so that God will love and accept them. It can also drive a person up the wall with obsessive fears of possibly committing the unpardonable sin. I have seen this many times, where people are harassed by irrational and compulsive blasphemous thoughts against the Holy Spirit and then condemned for being hopeless. It seems the more they fear committing it, the worse and more compulsive those thoughts become.

  Anybody who has fears of the unpardonable sin is pretty much guaranteed to have this stronghold. Anybody who can truly see God as the loving Father that He truly is will be virtually immune to fears of the unpardonable sin.
- It can cause people to find it hard to trust God. They may wonder if He will really come through for them as His Word promises. They would have a hard time giving up health insurance and a high-paying job and trusting God for those areas of their lives if God told them to do so.
- It can cause a tremendous amount of legalism in a person's life. Legalism is where a people are driven to do what's right because they feel they have to do it in order to win favor with God or keep Him satisfied with them. This is living according to the law and not the Spirit. The law of the Spirit is where people do what is right because they want to, not because they *have* to.

The three C's of cognitive behavior, which I use in my practice, come from the theory of cognitive behavior therapy. It is based on the idea that the way you see yourself, the world, and other people can affect your thoughts and feelings and can ultimately lead to mental health problems. With cognitive behavior therapy, clients are able to learn how to change the way they think and see themselves, which will in turn improve their psychological problems and their mental well-being. This form of psychotherapy treats problems and boosts the interpersonal happiness modifying dysfunctional emotions, behaviors, and thoughts.

Unlike traditional Freudian psychanalysis, which probes childhood wounds to get at the root causes of conflict, CBT focuses on solutions, encouraging the client or counselee to challenge distorted cognitions and change destructive patterns of behavior. I'd like to call this catch it, check it, and change it.

1. Catch it—thoughts. "For the weapons of our warfare are not carnal but mighty through God to the pulling down of strongholds." Spot when you might be having these kinds of negative thoughts. The best way to do this is probably to use your emotions as "cues." When you feel anxious or depressed, check your thoughts. What are you thinking? Could those thoughts make you depressed or anxious? Any negative thoughts need to be caught. Catch the negative thought. Learn to be aware of what you are thinking and when you have a negative thought. One of the defining factors of being human is the ability to analyze ourselves and our own thoughts.

2. Check it—emotions. "Casting down imaginations and every high thought that exalts itself against the knowledge of God." Stop and think about what you're thinking. Is it really true? Do you have evidence to back it up? Would other people interpret things in the same way? This is perhaps the most difficult part of the exercise, as nearly everybody believes his or her own thoughts are right (think about arguments with friends about politics or football). It's very difficult to check out your own thoughts objectively. That's why CBT is best done with a therapist, who is much more able to take that "one step back" perspective (there a few substeps to this one). It's difficult to be objective about one's thoughts, so it can be helpful to talk things over sometimes with someone else or with a therapist or psychiatrist.

   a. Be rational. Is it real? Examine the evidence. You can ask someone else about it. (Did you hear that? Did such-and-such happen? What do you think of this idea or theory?) Use logic.

   b. Be specific.

   c. Think in shades of gray. Often, things are not absolute. What are your strengths and weaknesses? What can you work on?

d. Apply the double-standard technique. With negative self-talk, we wouldn't usually talk to our friends or family the way we sometimes talk to ourselves (or think about ourselves). Try not to be too hard on yourself when working on this. It's not necessary to hold yourself to unachievable or unreachable higher standards when comparing yourself to others. It is a distorted thought thinking you are better than everyone else (or wanting to be better).

e. Now check all of this against the Word of God.

3. Change it—actions. "And bringing into captivity every thought into the obedience of Christ. At this point, you need to try substituting more realistic thoughts. If your automatic thoughts tend to be depressive or anxious, you need to think of differently—but realistically—about the situation. Then, check out these new ways of thinking. Are they more likely to be true than your automatic thoughts? Do they make you feel any different?

Disabilities Chart

THE 3 D'S—DELAY, DISTRACT, AND DECIDE

Delay works with catch it. You choose a time delay anywhere from five minutes to one hour. This really works well with counselees dealing with the stronghold of addiction.

Then you distract by doing something else. This goes with check it. When you distract, you can check the truth.

Lastly, you decide. This allows you to change it with the final decisions.

THE NEW ME

Practice makes perfect. Psychologists and psychiatrists have found that homework is important here. It's important to practice, so try using the following simple diary. There's an example version to show how you can use it. Print it off, and practice. Remember, this is a very difficult process. Overcoming mental health problems is a huge challenge, and even though CBT is probably the most effective approach, our catch it, check it, change it guide is just a very simple first step.

Mental illness is a tough thing to consider because it can open a debate that many would rather not have. But given the overwhelming response these past few weeks on my blog and in other spheres of social media, it bears discussing more fully before we close the conversation for now.

Among evangelicals, you will find some who are very open to dealing with mental illness as a physiological reality, but you will also find others who think that there is no other value to be gained from listening to the world. One might wonder why we can't just read enough Scripture or pray enough. Why can't that cure us? Because the reality is that in some cases, there are physical, chemical, or physiological issues. Yes, prayer can help, and yes, God does still heal in miraculous ways. But more often than not, more prayer and more faith are not the only remedy for mental illness. Medicine is still needed.

Most people would agree that in many ways, we are an overmedicated society. I don't deny that. But that is a separate discussion for another day. Just because we need to be careful in how we prescribe and administer medication does not mean we should be afraid of medical intervention entirely. And yes, mental health is a spiritual issue in some instances, but it can also be a medical issue. We have to recognize—and admit—that the faith community sometimes is unsure of how to deal with this tension. All truth is God's truth, and there are both spiritual truths and medical truths that are part of dealing with this issue.

Chapter 8

WHAT YOU EAT IMPACTS YOUR MENTAL HEALTH

Healthy diets (fruits, vegetables, fish, and so on) and unhealthy diets (starch, sweets, soda, and so on) were examined in order to see if they would be significant predictors of general mental health, happiness, optimism, and satisfaction with life levels while controlling for the possibly confounding variables of age, gender, alcohol, smoking, and social support. Initially, after using hierarchical multiple regression, the results showed that diet was a significant predictor of only optimism and happiness levels in participants; however, after controlling for the confounding variables, the relationship disappeared. In the final model, diet was not a significant predictor of general mental health, happiness, satisfaction with life, and optimism. The final analysis showed that age was the only significant predictor of all measures of mental health used, along with smoking status being a significant predictor of happiness, satisfaction with life, and optimism. Lastly, the degree of alcohol use was also a significant predictor of optimism levels. Future research should take into consideration the role of confounding variables in diet and nutrition research.

Nutrition has long been known as a gateway for physical health. According to Stein (2014), the importance of nutrition dates back to Hippocrates (400 BC), where he stated, "Let food be your medicine and medicine be your food." Essential nutrients include carbohydrates, proteins, fats, fiber, vitamins, minerals, and water. It has become common knowledge that getting the right amount and balance of these nutrients can have a huge impact on a person's overall physical health. According to Nicoletto and Rinaldi (2011), the nutrient supply of children in the womb is essential to later physical health and development, and a lack of nutrition at this time point could result in the later development of diseases, such as cardiovascular disease and diabetes.

It has also been noted by Stacey and Seidl (2014) that nutrition can play a part in preventing Parkinson's disease along with treating it. The study notes the importance of different nutrients and minerals and their role within the disease—specifically the role of the omega-3 fatty acid docosahexaenoic acid (fish and salad greens), which has been shown to be neuroprotective in terms of Parkinson's, as well as a deficiency in Vitamin D linked to disruption in homeostasis in the body, which may play a part in the development of Parkinson's. According to Ajmera (2013), poor nutrition, such as a high intake of fried foods, sugar, salt, and fast food, has also been linked to obesity, hypertension, heart disease, gout, and diabetes among other diseases, including cancer.

Psychological disorders such as depression, anxiety, hyperactivity, learning disorders, bipolar depression, manic depression, alcoholism, and schizophrenia can be treated quite successfully with diet and nutritional supplementation, as well as changes in lifestyle and improving air quality in the environment.

The brain is dependent on adequate supplies of nutrients in order to function properly. When it doesn't receive these nutrients, then the deficiency is exhibited in a variety of negative symptoms in thought, mood, emotion, perception, and behavior.

Mental health is deeply affected by the following factors:

- neurotransmitters
- pesticides and herbicides
- food allergies and sensitivities
- nutritional deficiencies
- *Candida* overgrowth
- hormone imbalances
- environmental toxins
- hypoglycemia—low blood sugar
- food additives and preservatives
- hypothyroidism—low thyroid
- sugar
- adrenal fatigue

I will have to cover these and their effects in a later discussion. However, given the preceding list, symptoms from these issues can range anywhere from mild melancholy to suicidal depression. They may include anxiety, outbursts of anger, autism, hyperactivity, schizophrenia and mania, obsessive-compulsive disorders, memory difficulties, learning disorders, drug and alcohol addiction, paranoia, and agoraphobia. For example, many people have found that eliminating dairy and wheat products from their diet can greatly reduce the symptoms associated with schizophrenia, hyperactivity, and autism.

While others have amazing results in relieving ADHD or hyperactivity, depression, autism, anxiety, and just about any psychological problem you can think of by following a *Candida* diet, ADHD diet, or Paleolithic diet and balancing neurotransmitters. And yet many other people have found relief from these same afflictions with supplementation of a variety of vitamins and minerals like B-complex, magnesium, amino acids, and fatty acids and getting adequate sunlight. Other alternative mental health methods may include cleaning up toxins from the environment, pinpointing food allergies and sensitivities that may exist, identifying any possible metabolic disorders, such as hypoglycemia or malfunctioning in organs like the thyroid and adrenals.

NUTRITION AND YOUR BRAIN

According to Logan (2007), although it is commonly known that nutrition plays a part in many physical ailments, such as cardiovascular disease and cancer, it is still less known that nutrition can also play a part in many mental conditions, such as depression, anxiety, ADHD, headaches, and Alzheimer's Disease. In light of this, investigating this issue further would be of use in order to find out the relationship our daily food habits have to our everyday mental well-being. According to Moser (2012), many of us are already aware that consuming low-nutrient foods, such as fat, sugar, fast food, and so on, can leave individuals feeling void of energy, obese, and in a depressed mood, and having a diet high in fruits, vegetables, and nuts can have the reverse effect. This statement is supported by a study done by Ruusunen (2013), where different dietary habits were investigated. It was found that diets rich in vegetables, fruits, berries, whole grains, and fish were good for decreasing the risk of depression and negative mental states. It also showed that a Western-culture diet rich in processed meats, chips, and soft drinks significantly increased an individual's risk of depression. From this research, it can be seen that there seems to be a relationship between food habits and an individual's subsequent mental health. In order to understand why specific diets impact upon mental health the way they do, it's important to understand how nutrients impact the functioning of the brain.

According to Leyse-Wallace (2013), nutrients, at whatever level in the body, whether that may be in excess, inadequate, or so on, can have a significant effect on the functioning of the brain and the central nervous system. A lack of nutrients can lead to consequences as severe as a deteriorated mental state or as simple as mild discomfort, such as the stress and irritability experienced when a caffeine addict does not get his or her morning coffee.

According to Schmidt (2007), the brain is made up of 60 percent fat. New research in the area has outlined the importance of the types of fats and oils we put into our bodies and the way they can affect the efficient functioning of the brain. The ingestion of essential fatty acids and omega-3 and 6 can have effects on our mental health as young as the gestation period, all the way through until old age. Lacking these essential minerals has been linked to abnormal functioning of the brain, such as bipolar disorder, depression, memory loss, Alzheimer's, and even poor social skills. Overall, it was stated that fatty acids are essential in order to manage the brain's complex structure.

These fatty acids must be consumed in our diets because the brain cannot generate them itself. Fatty acids are essentially building blocks of the brain that if not supplied to the brain can cause significant mental health decline. According to Davison (2012), nutrition is essential in the maintenance and efficient workings of the brain. This happens through the interconnection of many nutrients. Some examples of these nutrients and their functions within the brain include carbohydrates, which are linked with glucose, the energy source of the brain; vitamin B3, which is linked with the production of dopamine; and vitamin C, which acts as an antioxidant within the brain and is neuroprotective. A lack of vitamin E has also been linked to Alzheimer's disease.

There has also been research into which parts of the brain these nutrients work with and how they can affect the emotional stability of individuals. For example, there seems to be a connection between nutrition and stress. According to Talbott (2007), high cortisol levels due to prolonged or high stress periods in a person's life can cause negative effects on a person's overall mental health, as well as being associated with the subsequent development of depressive symptoms. According to the same source, there is a specific enzyme named HSD (11 beta-hydroxysteroid dehydrogenase), which is associated with higher cortisol levels in the body. A natural way in which to inhibit the activation of this enzyme was higher ingestion of things such as fruits, herbs, and vegetables. Most notably are foods such as apples, onions, grapefruit, and soybeans, which are high in flavonoids. Flavonoids combat HSD levels.

Another mental condition that may have a source in nutrition is anxiety. Anxiety is one of the most common mental illnesses in today's world. According to Baxter et al. (2013), the worldwide prevalence is 28.3 percent. In a study done by Lakhan and Vieira (2010), herbs and nutrition play a role in anxiety. In their research, they outlined the importance of food high in magnesium, such as beans, nuts, wholegrain foods, and green leafy vegetables. They also outlined the essential benefits that herbs, such as passionflower or kava, can play in our diets to promote positive mental health. Their study showed that subjects who stuck to these nutritional diet guidelines suffered from less anxiety than before commencing the diet; however, there was a question about whether this was due to a placebo effect.

It was also found that caffeine plays a role in anxiety symptoms (Childs et al., 2008).

Depression is also a mental condition that is extremely common and can effect everybody at least once in their lifetime. There are many treatments for depression, such as psychotherapy and drug treatments. However, even though there are many treatments available for a very common disorder, none seem to be adequate enough in sustaining relapse in patients. Could nutrition play a role in preventing and treating depression? A study done by Coppen et al. (2005) stated that there may be a role for nutrition in the prevention and treatment of depression. Folic acid and vitamin B12 were outlined as being very important. In the research, there was found to be a link between folic acid and antidepressant response rates, as well as Vitamin B12 being associated with better treatment outcomes. Both of these nutrients are associated with adenosylmethionine, which is essential in efficient neurological functioning.

Nutrients are very important when it comes to the efficient and healthy workings of the brain. But in what ways are they important, and what are the specific diets that contribute to specific moods and behaviors? This is an essential starting point. Many people the world over follow different dietary habits for many different reasons, such as moral reasons, cultural norms, and health reasons, like diabetes. Let's take a more in-depth look at different diets that people adopt.

One phenomenon worth investigating is the potential effects of individuals who follow a vegetarian diet due to moral or health reasons. Vegetarians are identified as abstaining from eating meat and fish. It is a diet that has been gaining popularity in the last decade and has been linked with many health benefits, such as reduced cancer rates, lower mortality, and better cholesterol levels (Nordqvist, 2014). However, many research studies studying the impact of vegetarianism on mental health have correlated it negatively with positive mental health.

A diet completely opposite to vegetarianism is a ketogenic diet, which has long been investigated and promoted in treating individuals who suffer from epilepsy. It is a high-protein and low-carbohydrate diet that forces the body to burn fats rather than carbohydrates.

According to Mallakh R. S., Paskitti M. E. (2001) and Phelps J. R., Siemers S. V., El-Mallakh R. S. (2013), a ketogenic diet has been associated with the reduction of bipolar symptoms by inhibiting executory neurons in the brain and found to be correlated with a more positive mind frame. However the studies included extremely small sample sizes and may be at risk of the placebo effect, as the participants were noted as really wanting the diet to work and being extremely motivated for it to do so. In this way, the studies may be biased and further investigation will be needed in the area.

Clearly, there is support for the idea that a diet rich in vegetables, fruit, fish, whole foods, nuts, and so on has a positive impact on mental health. Unfortunately, in the last decade, the consumption of processed, sugary, and fatty foods has dramatically increased. The growth of popularity of cheap, processed, high-fat, high-sugar, high-salt foods and so on has been a major problem in the last fifty years. According to De Vogli R, Kouvonen A, Gimeno D. 'Globesization' (2013), the amount of annual fast food transactions per capita between 1999 and 2008 has increased from 26.61 percent to 32.76 percent. The study involved twenty-seven high-income countries. Fast food and processed foods are generally extremely high in salt content, which has been linked to later decline of cognitive functioning, especially when combined with inactivity (Brooks, 2011). Processed foods also tend to be extremely high in sugar. A study done by Peet (2004) found that consuming a diet high in sugar was highly correlated with levels of schizophrenia and depression. This seems to be due to a key brain hormone called BDNF. High sugar suppresses the growth of this hormone, which in low volumes has been associated with depression and schizophrenia. Secondly, high levels of sugar can cause inflammation in the body, which can disrupt the immune system and the efficient working of the brain, which again, has been linked to depression and schizophrenia.

The idea that a Western diet high in processed foods, fat, sugar, and salt and low in organic fruit and vegetables and so on can wreak havoc on your brain and essential mood and behavior has been supported by a study done by Green (2003), where it was found that people of the Arctic have been in increasingly more contact with the Western world and results showed that there has been an increase in mental health problems, such as anxiety, depression, and even suicide in the Arctic society.

Overall, there has been a general decline in consumption of foods rich in nutrients that have been shown to have a significant impact on the mental health of an individual. Specifically, there has been a general decline in the consumption of fruits, vegetables, and fish, with individuals having a higher and higher preference for quick, easy, low-nutrition, fast food. According to Popkin BM, Nielsen SJ (2012), since the turn of the millennium, there has been a major increase in Western society in consumption of refined carbohydrates, sugars, fats, oils, and sweeteners and a major reduction in the consumption of vegetables, grains, and fruits.

My final words on the topic of nutrition have a lot to do with our mental health. Mental health disorders are rising in children and being referred to as an epidemic. Numerous studies have shown micronutrient deficiencies and poor diet quality are suspected of playing a contributory role in the escalation of certain disorders. However, there is no research in young children focusing specifically on social-emotional disorders and possible links to nutrition. Conventional treatment for social-emotional disorders in children typically involves medication. Parents are increasingly turning to complementary and alternative medicine to treat their children with a method that is individualized and holistic. The biopsychosocial model provided the theoretical framework for this correlational study that investigated the association between nutrient intake and social-emotional functioning. Multiple regression analyses were conducted to determine if diet/health indicators were significant predictors of any of the subscale scores on the *Behavior Assessment System for Children—Second Edition (BASC-2), Parent Rating Scale—Preschool* social-emotional variables. Intake of food categories was measured by the amount reported by a sample of 119 parents over a three-day period. Higher levels of processed food consumption significantly predicted higher scores of atypicality. Additionally, reporting a family history of mental illness was associated with lower levels of hyperactivity and depression.

The relationships between the other diet quality and health indicators and social-emotional functioning in children were nonsignificant. The results of this study offer an alternative or supplemental treatment modality to psychotropic drugs. With the increasing health and economic burden of mental health disorders in children, the investigation of risk factors such as nutrient intake is an essential and pressing research initiative.

As I have examined the relationship between nutrient intake and social-emotional functioning in mental health, I conclude that nutrient intake is important for mental health, particularly the development of atypicality. It is evident that in the treatment of mood disorders, factors of importance include the assessment of nutrient intake. Well-designed, rigorous studies are needed to determine if poor nutrition contributes to psychosocial functioning in children. There is a growing interest in alternative interventions for preschool children with disorders such as ADHD, but the efficacy of such treatments must be evaluated through various research studies. Understanding the relationship between nutrient intake and social-emotional functioning will promote improvements in offering intervention services by mental health providers and medical professionals.

You can imagine your brain on food, and it's always on. Your brain takes care of your thoughts and movements, your breathing and heartbeat, your senses—it works hard twenty-four/seven, even while you're asleep. This means your brain requires a constant supply of fuel. That "fuel" comes from the foods you eat—and what's in that fuel makes all the difference. Put simply, what you eat directly affects the structure and function of your brain and, ultimately, your mood.

Like an expensive car, your brain functions best when it gets only premium fuel. Eating high-quality foods that contain lots of vitamins, minerals, and antioxidants nourishes the brain and protects it from oxidative stress the "waste" (free radicals) produced when the body uses oxygen, which can damage cells.

Unfortunately, just like an expensive car, your brain can be damaged if you ingest anything other than premium fuel. If substances from "low-premium" fuel (such as what you get from processed or refined foods) gets to the brain, it has little ability to get rid of them. Diets high in refined sugars, for example, are harmful to the brain. In addition to worsening your body's regulation of insulin, they also promote inflammation and oxidative stress. Multiple studies have found a correlation between a diet high in refined sugars and impaired brain function and even a worsening of symptoms of mood disorders, such as depression.

It makes sense. If your brain is deprived of good-quality nutrition, or if free radicals or damaging inflammatory cells are circulating within the brain's enclosed space, further contributing to brain tissue injury, consequences are to be expected. What's interesting is that for many years, the medical field did not fully acknowledge the connection between mood and food.

Studies have shown that when people take probiotics (supplements containing the good bacteria), their anxiety levels, perception of stress, and mental outlook improve, compared with people who did not take probiotics. Other studies have compared "traditional" diets, like the Mediterranean diet and the traditional Japanese diet, to a typical "Western" diet and have shown that the risk of depression is 25 to 35 percent lower in those who eat a traditional diet. Scientists account for this difference because these traditional diets tend to be high in vegetables, fruits, unprocessed grains, and fish and seafood and to contain only modest amounts of lean meats and dairy. They are also void of processed and refined foods and sugars, which are staples of the "Western" dietary pattern. In addition, many of these unprocessed foods are fermented and therefore act as natural probiotics. Fermentation uses bacteria and yeast to convert sugar in food to carbon dioxide, alcohol, and lactic acid. It is used to protect food from spoiling and can add a pleasant taste and texture.

HEALTHY DIET: EATING WITH MENTAL HEALTH IN MIND

You've probably heard the expression, "You are what you eat," but what exactly does that mean? Put simply, food is fuel, and the kinds of foods and drinks you consume determine the types of nutrients in your system and impact how well your mind and body are able to function.

Drinks

Avoid sugary drinks and excessive amounts of caffeine. Sugary drinks have empty calories and damage tooth enamel. Caffeine should also be avoided in excess, as it can trigger panic attacks in people who have anxiety disorders.

Try to drink at least eight glasses of water a day (about two liters) to prevent dehydration. Studies show that even mild dehydration can cause fatigue, difficulty concentrating, and mood changes, in addition to physical effects like thirst, decreased or dark urine, dry skin, headache, dizziness, and constipation. Limit caffeine if you have an anxiety disorder. If you feel like you need some caffeine, try tea. Tea has lower amounts of caffeine than coffee and has lots of antioxidants—chemicals found in plants that protect body tissues and prevent cell damage.

Breakfast

Avoid skipping breakfast. You need breakfast to fuel your body (including your brain) after going without food during sleep, and it also jump-starts your metabolism for the day. Skipping meals leads to fatigue and feelings of "brain fog."

Try to incorporate a healthy breakfast into your routine. If you're tight on time in the mornings, grab a whole-grain granola bar, yogurt, and a piece of fruit to get you off to a good start.

LUNCH AND DINNER

Avoid high-fat dairy and fried, refined, and sugary foods, which have little nutritional value. In addition to contributing to weight gain and conditions like diabetes, research shows that a diet that consists primarily of these kinds of foods significantly increases the risk of depression. Try to eat a diet that relies on fruits, vegetables, nuts, whole grains, fish, and unsaturated fats (like olive oil). People who follow this kind of diet are up to 30 percent less likely to develop depression than people who eat lots of meat and dairy products. Find more information on http://www.mentalhealthamerica.net/conditions/healthy-diet-eating-mental-health-mind.

UNDERSTANDING THE LINK BETWEEN
SUBSTANCE ABUSE AND MENTAL ILLNESS

Understanding the link between substance abuse and mental illness is a concern for mental health providers, social workers, and anyone in the medical field working with individuals who have a dual diagnosis. Any individual whose goal is to improve the support and treatment for individuals with a dual diagnosis should be knowledgeable of the range of problems that require a range of solutions. Drake, Mercer-McFadden, Mueser, McHugo, and Bond (1998) assert that an integrated approach is not only necessary but crucial to treat both the drug addiction and mental illness concurrently. Focusing on only one disorder would be a disservice to the individual. Drake, R. M., Mercer-McFadden, C., Mueser, K.T., McHugo, G.J., and Bond, G.R. (1998) ascertains that the ramifications of dually diagnosed clients not being treated concurrently for drug addiction and mental illness can greatly affect their ability to combat their addiction and take control of their mental illness. Dual diagnosis presents a problem in the mental health and medical field. Generally, patients may present issues to their primary-care physician (Phillips, McKeown, and Sandford, 2010) first allowing for an early opportunity to ascertain if an individual is suffering from a mental health and substance abuse condition.

Medical, mental, and substance history can be reviewed to ascertain if the client has a cooccurring disorder. The client can then be referred to an appropriate treatment program. According to Carey and Correia (1998), substance abuse is often overlooked and underdiagnosed in the mental health setting. Mental health staff may lack training or may be inexperienced when diagnosing substance abuse in patients. Inadequate assessments can lead to an inappropriate treatment plan. Mueser, Drake, and Wallach (1998) contend individuals suffering from mental illness are at an increased risk for substance abuse.

According to NAMI.org (2015), one-third of people suffering from mental illness and half of the people with severe mental illness experience substance abuse. One-third of alcohol abusers and one-half of all drug abusers report that they have experienced mental illness. In other words, people with mental illness abuse drugs and people who abuse drugs suffer from mental illness. In order to effectively diagnose and treat people with a cooccurring disorder, one must first understand the link between mental illness and substance abuse. Without understanding the relationship between the two and the importance of treating both disorders simultaneously, treatment will not be as effective. Not only should mental health professionals be trained but medical personnel should also be trained to provide a line of defense. Patients should be screened by various medical professionals in case they do not originally seek help in a mental health setting.

In order to effectively screen and treat cooccurring disorders, it is necessary to have a system that can not only treat cooccurring disorders but intervene early enough so that clients receive adequate care. An intricate system of medical professionals, mental health professionals, and line staff who are adequately trained to recognize signs of substance abuse in those persons presenting with a cooccurring illness is needed to successfully treat those suffering from a dual diagnosis.

Cooccurring disorders affect those presenting with a mental illness and substance abuse problem. The combinations of mental disorders and the degree of mental functioning coupled with substance abuse requires a specialized approach. In a study by American Addiction Centers in 2019 used statistical information collected from residents currently receiving residential in-patient treatment at a facility servicing men and women that offered a dual-diagnosis approach for combating drug addiction and mental illness. Residents were asked to complete a simple survey consisting of eight questions. Each resident was asked his or her age, gender, ethnicity, the number of times he or she had sought treatment for mental health, the number of times treatment had been sought for substance use addiction, the number of relapses he or she believed he or she had suffered before entering the current facility, how many times the person had received concurrent treatment for both substance use and mental health, and which treatment program he or she felt was most beneficial to his or her recovery. The resident's responses to the mental-health- and substance-abuse-related questions determined whether concurrent treatment of substance abuse and mental health made a difference in the number of relapses that he or she suffered.

Social workers and mental health professionals need to be able to recognize cooccurring disorders in individuals they are treating. Watkins et al. (2004) report that increasing episodes of substance abuse is associated with a mental health condition. The high rate of cooccurring disorders should lead to social workers and mental health professionals being more equipped to handle those suffering from dual diagnosis. Di Lorenzo, Galliani, Guicciardi, Landi, and Ferri (2014) assert that the clinical and rehabilitative needs of patients with a cooccurring disorder are different and depend on the patient's level of functioning, which is conditioned by his or her pathological behavior and poor compliance with therapy. If social workers and mental health care professionals become properly trained in the diagnosis of those suffering from dual diagnoses, it can greatly enhance the well-being of those who suffer from cooccurring disorders.

No one can exactly say which came first: drug addiction or mental illness. An integrated approach is best to combat this twofold problem. The disorders cannot be treated separately, as they occur within the same person. Properly treating individuals with a cooccurring disorder will allow them to function in society as a whole. By focusing on the relationship between substance abuse and mental illness, health-care professionals can focus on screening tools, effective interventions, and continuous support. An integrated treatment approach consists of programs that encompasses the treatment of drug addiction and mental illness concurrently.

When I think of the Bible and the war that goes in the mind of the counselee or client, I look more closely at the Word of God for my answers—which brings me to the holistic way to treat mental illness. The holistic model of health care is based on treating the "whole" person, taking into consideration the mental, emotional, physical, social, and spiritual states of well-being. Unlike traditional medicine (or "allopathic medicine"), which addresses the symptoms of a condition or disease, holistic medical practitioners evaluate the patient's complete health picture and examine how all body systems interrelate before determining a plan for healing. I have found that in recent years, more and more people whose chronic ailments have been unsuccessfully treated by allopathic medicine are considering holistic medicine. Certainly modern medicine has its merits, but the main purpose of surgery and medications is to attack illness rather than create health.

Holistic medicine is more preventive in nature than allopathic medicine; it strives to help the body achieve balance and optimal health, prevent disease, and decipher the true source of an illness or condition. Thus, holistic therapies are especially helpful to people with the ability and desire to be proactive in their healing—hence getting the body mind soul and spirt back to the place where God intended.

Mental well-being can be improved and enhanced by an array of natural, holistic modalities that range from acupuncture to art therapy. The holistic model supports the idea that body chemistry, spirituality, diet, nutrition, and other factors can impact the brain in diverse ways. Holistic mental health may indeed include your basic talk therapy, but it also looks beyond that and connects with other alternative mental health therapies like diet, nutrition, and changes in lifestyle to achieve optimal psychological functioning. It emphasizes the interconnectedness of the body, mind, and spirit and utilizes methods outside the realm of conventional psychotherapy.

Unlike traditional psychiatry, instead of medicating the brain with toxic drugs, it attempts to find the underlying cause of the psychological symptom that is exhibited. Mainstream medicine or psychology has a very limited understanding and knowledge of the role of brain chemistry in mental health and the impact of diet, nutrition, and chemicals in the environment on the brain.

The physiological and psychological have a profound impact on one another. Good mental health can't exist without attending to the physical and spiritual matters and vice versa, and it also can't exist without balancing brain chemistry.

Holistic mental health addresses psychological problems from the biochemical angle. Although both mainstream psychology and alternative therapies understand that neurotransmitters are at the root of all mental health conditions, mainstream psychology attempts to fix these problems with medication, and we attempt to fix them with diet, nutritional supplements, and changes in lifestyle.

In the biochemical approach, there is no such thing as "mental" illness in and of itself. Any so-called "mental illness" can always be linked to something physiological as the root cause. Mental disorders, conditions, illnesses, and so on are the result of biochemical disorders with symptoms that exhibit in the psychological arena. What appears to be a psychological symptom is really triggered by something in the body chemistry or environmental sources, such as pesticides, foods, or other chemicals.

Tyler Woods, PhD, a Tucson-based holistic health practitioner, explains that holistic mental health care stands "outside the realm of traditional care," with practitioners demonstrating a willingness to look outside the box when treating a patient's mental condition. Woods believes that the best practitioners are thorough and ask patients the right questions in order to help them seek the most beneficial courses of treatment. After twenty years of working with clients in the social services field, Woods retired as a psychotherapist in 2004 and opened the Mindhance Wellness Center. The catalyst for Woods's shift was her realization that the root of her depression was undiagnosed diabetes, a condition she believes a holistic practitioner might have discovered earlier.[1]

Physical illness and psychological symptoms are often caused by imbalances in the body. A common contributor to mental health conditions such as irritability, depression, anxiety, and ADHD is a poor diet. Years of consuming the wrong foods can create allergies and sensitivities, nutritional deficiencies, *Candida* overgrowth, hypoglycemia (low blood sugar), and hormonal imbalances, all of which can impair healthy brain function. The brain requires a regular supply of adequate nutrients. Without these nutrients, one's emotions, perception, and behavior can be affected. One may develop symptoms mild to severe— that range from simple melancholy to anxiety, autism, hyperactivity, obsessive-compulsive conditions, learning problems, drug and alcohol addiction, and even schizophrenia.

Eight key factors that may cause or intensify mental health conditions are as follows:

---

[1] http://mypassion4health.com/articles/mental_wellness/.

1. Blood toxicity, resulting from heavy metals or environmental chemicals (especially lead and mercury)
2. Improper diet, particularly poor quality or processed foods or foods containing wheat, gluten, sugar, artificial sweeteners, and dairy products (to which many people are highly sensitive)
3. Lack of exercise
4. Drug and alcohol use and abuse
5. Hormonal or chemical imbalances in the body
6. Psychological factors, including traumatic events, prolonged untreated stress, self-destructive beliefs, serious financial hardships, and so on
7. Genetics, as evidenced by a family history of mental health conditions or hormonal imbalances
8. Lack of support from family, community, or spiritual groups

This was part of my training, and I have added this in my practice of mental health as well. I have also taken this into the classroom and practice the effectiveness of holistic mental health through *mindfulness*. The Georgia Department of Mental Health had a conference in October 2017. I was an attendant at this conference. It was on *mindfulness* and holistic rehabilitation therapy. I took this further and wanted to see how this would work with regular clients when I used music therapy as a form of treatment of depression, anxiety, and mental toughness.

Given the extensive evidence base for the efficacy of mindfulness-based stress reduction (MBSR) and mindfulness-based cognitive therapy (MBCT), researchers have started to explore the mechanisms underlying their therapeutic effects on psychological outcomes, using methods of mediation analysis. No known studies have systematically reviewed and statistically integrated mediation studies in this field. The present study aimed to systematically review mediation studies in the literature on mindfulness-based interventions (MBIs), to identify potential psychological mechanisms underlying MBCT's and MBSR's effects on psychological functioning and well-being and evaluate the strength and consistency of evidence for each mechanism. For the identified mechanisms with sufficient evidence, quantitative synthesis using two-stage meta-analytic structural equation modelling (TSSEM) was used to examine whether these mechanisms mediate the impact of MBIs on clinical outcomes.

Conclusion

From my research, I have found that there is a spiritual war going on in the mind of an individual. The Bible states,

> If any of you lacks wisdom, he should ask God, who gives generously to all without finding fault, and it will be given to him. But when he asks, he must believe and not doubt, because he who doubts is like a wave of the sea, blown and tossed by the wind. That man should not think he will receive anything from the Lord; he is a double-minded man, unstable in all he does. (James 1:5–7 NIV).

In Joyce Meyer's book *The Battlefield of the Mind*, she uses the passage of Scripture from Ephesians 6:12 (AMP):

> For we are not wrestling with flesh and blood [contending only with physical opponents], but against the despotisms, against the powers, against [the master spirits who are] the world rulers of this present darkness, against the spirit forces of wickedness in the heavenly (supernatural) Sphere.

From this scripture, we see that we are in a war. A careful study of this verse informs us that our warfare is not with other human beings but with the devil and his demons. Our enemy, Satan, attempts to defeat us with strategy and deceit, through well-laid plans and deliberate deception. Satan bombards the mind of the client with little nagging thoughts, suspicions, doubts, fears, wonderings, reasonings, and theories. He moves slowly and cautiously (after all, well-laid plans take time). Remember, he has a strategy for his warfare.

He has studied us for a long time. He knows what we like and what we don't like. He knows our insecurities, our weaknesses, and our fears. He knows what bothers us most. He is willing to invest any amount of time it takes to defeat us. One of the devil's strong points is patience.

When you live with a mental illness, you fight a lifelong battle. When you're medicated, staying away from booze and drugs and doing other things to take care of yourself (sleep, exercise, and so on), you're winning the battle. The mental illness cannot control you, because you have learned to control it. But when you don't do those things, and unfortunately sometimes even when you do, the mental illness begins to regain control, and you start to suffer. That's when the demons come out.

Everyone has demons, mental illness or not, but these types of demons are different; they can convince you to believe their lies. Their lies are different for everyone. They tell you things like that you are worthless, and you don't deserve to be happy. They tell you that life is too hard, and you should stop trying. They bombard you with horrible lies, and sometimes you start to believe them. That's when you have to reach for help. Call your doctor or counselor or someone you trust, because sometimes it's just too hard to do it alone. Unfortunately, not everyone knows how to ask for help.

Those who are suffering from depression or other mental illnesses try to drown out their demons with alcohol or silence them with drugs, but that just gives the demons more power. If you're medicated, alcohol and drugs cancel out all the good that medication does and actually begin to make everything worse. When the mental illness gains full control, when the demons overpower you, you feel there's no end to this. Always remember the words of Paul in 2 Cor.10:3–5 (NKJV):

> For though we live in the world, we do not wage war as the world does. The weapons we fight with are not the weapons of the world. On the contrary, they have divine power to demolish strongholds. We demolish arguments and every pretension that sets itself up against the knowledge of God, and we take captive every thought to make it obedient to Christ.

Mental health can be considered as a stronghold. Strongholds can be a source of protection for us from the devil, as is the case when the Lord becomes our stronghold, as He did for David. Or a stronghold can be a source of defense for the devil's influence in our lives, where demonic or sinful activity is actually defended within our sympathetic thoughts toward evil. I'm not implying that mental illness is demonic and cast out with prayer and exorcism. This was believed in days of old. However, some are, and they are forces that we deal with in our clients and counselees. Mental illness is a chemical imbalance within the human brain.

Works Cited

Ajmera, R. (2013, October 21). "The Effects of Poor Nutrition on Your Health." Retrieved from http://www.livestrong.com/article/31172-effectspoor-nutrition-health/.

"Any Anxiety Disorder among Adults." (n.d.). Retrieved January 16, 2015. http://www.nimh.nih.gov/health/statistics/prevalence/any-anxiety-disorder-among-adults.shtml.

APA. (2013). *Diagostic and Statistical Manual of Mental Disorders*. Fifth Ed. Washington, DC: American Psychiatric Publishing Co.

"Bipolar Disorder among Adults." (n.d.). Retrieved January 16, 2015. http://www.nimh.nih.gov/health/statistics/prevalence/bipolar-disorder-among-adults.shtml.

Brooks, M. (2011, September 6). "Salt and Inactivity: A Recipe for Cognitive Decline." Retrieved from http://www.medscape.com/viewarticle/749178.

Carey, K. B., and Correia, C.J. (1998). Severe mental illness and addictions: Assessment considerations. Addictive Behaviors, 23(6), 735- 748. doi:10.1016/S0306-4603(98)00063-X

Childs, E., C. Hohoff, J. Deckert, K. Xu, J. Badner, and H. De Wit. (2008). "Association between ADORA2A and DRD2 Polymorpisms and Caffeine-Induced Anxiety." *Neuropsychopharmacology* 33, no. 12: 2791–800. Retrieved from http://www.ncbi.nlm.nih.gov/pubmed/18305461.

Coppen, A. and C. Bolander-Gouaille. (2005). "Treatment of Depression: Time to Consider Folic Acid and Vitamin B12." *Journal of Psychopharmacology* 19, no. 1: 59–65. Retrieved from http://www.ncbi.nlm.nih.gov/pubmed/15671130.

Corey, G. (2001). *Theory and Practice of Counseling and Psychotherapy*. Belmont, CA: Brooks/Cole Thomson.

Davidson R. (2017) Neuroscience of Compassion. Teaneck NJ: Better Listen LLC.

"Depressive Disorders." (2015). *Psychology Today.* (January 21). https://www.psychologytoday.com/us/conditions/depressive-disorders

De Vogli R, Kouvonen A, Gimeno D. 'Globesization': ecological evidence on the relationship between fast food outlets and obesity among 26 advanced economies. Crit Public Health. 2011;21:395–402. doi: 10.1080/09581596.2011.619964.

Di Lorenzo, R. G., A. Galliani, A. Guicciardi, G. Landi, and P. Ferri. (2014). "A Retrospective Analysis Focusing on a Group of Patients with Dual Diagnosis Treated by Both Mental Health and Substance Use Services." *Neuropsychiatric Disease and Treatment* 10: 1479–1488. doi:10.2147/NDT.S65896.

Diagnostic and Statistical Manual of Mental Disorders—Text Revision. (2008). Arlington, VA: American Psychiatric Publishing, 419–420.

Drake, R. M., C. Mercer-McFadden, K. T. Mueser, G. J. McHugo, and G. R. Bond. (1998). "Review of Integrated Mental Health and Substance Abuse Treatment for Patients with Dual Disorders." *Schizophrenia Bulletin* 24, no. 4: 589–608. doi: 10.1093/oxfordjournals.schbul.a033351.

El-Mallakh R. S., Paskitti M. E. (2001). The ketogenic diet may have mood-stabilizing properties. Med. Hypotheses 57 (6), 724–726.

Gillies, D., S. JKH, S. S. Lad, M. J. Leach, and M. J. Ross. (2012). "Polyunsaturated Fatty Acids (PUFA) for Attention Deficit Hyperactivity Disorder (ADHD) in Children and Adolescents." *Cochrane Database Syst Rev* 7.

House, S.H. (2009). "Schoolchildren, Maternal Nutrition, and Generating Healthy Brains: The Importance of Lifecycle Education for Fertility, Health, and Peace." *Nutritional Health* 20: 51–76.

Jung, K., S. Ock, J. Chung, and C. Song. (2010). "Associations of Cerum Ca and Mg Levels with Mental Health in Adult Women without Psychiatric Disorders." *Biol Trace Elem* 107 Res, 133: 153–161.

Lemma, A. (1996). *Introduction to Psychopathology.* Thousand Oaks, CA: Sage Publications.

Logan, A. (2007) *"The Brain Diet: The Connection Between Nutrition, Mental Health, and Intelligence"* Nashville TN: Cumberland House Publishing

"Major Depression among Adults." (n.d.). Retrieved January 16, 2015. http://www.nimh.nih.gov/health/statistics/prevalence/major-depression-among-adults.shtml.

McGrath, Patrick, Ashan Khan, Madhukar Trivedi, Jonathan Stewart, David W. Morris, Stephen Wisniewski, Sachiko Miyahara, Andrew Nierenberg, Maurizio Fava, and John Rush (2008). "Response to a Selective Serotonin Reuptake Inhibitor (Citalopram) in Major Depressive Disorder with Melancholic Features: A STAR*D Report." *Journal of Clinical Psychiatry* 69: 1847–1855. doi:10.4088/jcp.v69n1201.

Mohr,W.K (2006) Spiritual Issues in Psychiatric Care Volume 42,Issue 3

Moser, I. (2012) *"How nd When to Be Your Own Doctor"* (Kindle Edtion)

Mueser, K. T., Drake, R.E., and Wallach, M.A. (1998). Dual diagnosis: A review of Etiological Theories. Addictive Behaviors, 23(6), 717-734. doi:10.1016/S0306-4603(98)00073-2

NAMI. (2014, November 27). Retrieved from the National Alliance on Mental Illness: http://www.nami.org.

Phelps J. R., Siemers S. V., El-Mallakh R. S. (2013). The ketogenic diet for type II bipolar disorder. Neurocase 19 (5), 423–426.

Phillips, P., O. McKeown, and T. Sandford, eds. (2009). *Dual Diagnosis: Practice in Context*. Ames, IA: John Wiley & Sons.

Popkin BM, Nielsen SJ. The sweetening of the world's diet. Obes Res. 2003;11:1325–1332.

Reardon, S. (2013). "Suicidal Behavior Is a Disease, Psychiatrists Argue." *New Scientist*. Retrieved March 13, 2014, from http://www.newscientist.com/article/dn23566-suicidal-behaviour-is-a disease-psychiatrists-argue.html.

Ruusunen A, 2013 - Diet and Depression: An Epidemiological Study.

University of Eastern Finland, Dissertations in Health Sciences, No 185 "Schizophrenia." (n.d.). Retrieved January 16, 2015.

Schmidt M.A. (2007*) Nutrition: How Dietary Fats and Oils Affect Mental, Physical, and Emotional Intellige* (3rd Edition) Berkeley, CA: North Atlantic Books

Stein, N.(2014) *" Public Health Nutrition : Principles and Practice for Community and Global Health"* Burlington, MA: Jones and Bartlett Learnin LLC.

Substance Abuse and Mental Health Services Administration. (2015). *Results from the 2014 National Survey on Drug Use and Health: Mental Health Findings*. NSDUH Series H-50, HHS Publication No. (SMA) 15-4927. Rockville, MD: Substance Abuse and Mental Health Services Administration. Retrieved October 27, 2015. http://www.samhsa.gov/data/sites/default/files/NSDUH-FRR1-2014/NSDUH-FRR1-2014.pdf.

Talboot,S.M (2007). The cortisol connection: why stress makes you fat and ruins your health--and what you can do about it 2nd ed. Alameda, CA: Hunter House

US Department of Housing and Urban Development, Office of Community Planning and Development. (2011). *The 2010 Annual Homeless Assessment Report to Congress*. Retrieved January 16, 2015. https://www.hudexchange.info/resources/documents/2010HomelessAssessmentRe.

Wallace, R.L.(2013) *Nutrition and Mental Health* Boca Raton, FL: CRC Press

Watkins, K., S. B. Hunter, S. L. Wenzel, W. Tu, S. M. Paddock, A. Griffin, and P. Ebener. (2004). "Prevalence and Characteristics of Clients with Cooccurring Disorders in Outpatient Substance Abuse Treatment." *American Journal of Drug and Alcohol Abuse* 30, no. 4: 749–764. doi:10.1081/ADA-200037538.

Webster's Collegiate Dictionary. Eleventh Edition. 2015

http://downloads.bbc.co.uk/headroom/cbt/catch_it.pdf

http://www.autismspeaks.org/family-services/epilepsy

http://www.autismspeaks.org/news/news-item/new-data-shows-half-all-children-autism-wander-and-bolt-safe-places

http://www.autismspeaks.org/what-autism

http://www.latuda.com

http://www.newsweek.com/nearly-1-5-americans-suffer-mental-illness-each-year-230608

https://www.nimh.nih.gov/health/statistics/index.shtml January 2018

http://www.nimh.nih.gov/health/statistics/prevalence/schizophrenia.shtml May 2018

http://www.nimh.nih.gov/health/topics/autism-spectrum-disorders-pervasive-developmental-disorders/index.shtml March 2018

http://www.thementalhealthsolution.com/mentalhealthtopics/hallucinations.html

https://www.ministrybooks.org/books.cfm?xid=YOSNN5VYZCPC4

https://www.nami.org/Learn-More/Mental-Health-By-the-Numbers

https://www.psychologytoday.com/blog/why-we-worry/201412/spirit-possession-and-mental-health Dec 31, 2014 Graham C. L. Davey, Ph.Dhttps://www.rpmministries.org/2014/01/is-cognitive-behavioral-therapy-the-same-as-biblical-mindheart-renewal/ Published on January 29, 2014 Dr. Bob Kellemen

https://www.ncbi.nlm.nih.gov/pmc/articles/PMC7768824/

East Asian Psychiatry. 2014 June 24 (2):58-67

Printed in the United States
By Bookmasters